THE SPIRITUAL ROOTS OF YOGA

Ages have passed turning the beads,
but turning of the heart has not occured,
Put aside the beads of the hand,
and turn the beads of the heart.

—*Kabir*

THE SPIRITUAL ROOTS OF YOGA

Royal Path to Freedom

RAVI RAVINDRA

Edited by
PRISCILLA MURRAY

The Spiritual Roots of Yoga

ISBN: 978-81-7822-365-0

First Indian Edition: Delhi, 2010
(First Edition published by Morning Light Press 2006)

Published by
NEW AGE BOOKS
A-44, Naraina Industrial Area, Phase-I
New Delhi (India)-110 028
Email: nab@vsnl.in
Website: www.newagebooksindia.com

Printed in India
at Shri Jainendra Press
A-45 Naraina Indl. Area, Phase-I, New Delhi-110 028

Dedicated to the sages
who have explored the Mystery
with steadfast attention and unsparing effort,
going from insight to insight
and from delight to delight.

Contents

Acknowledgments

Some essays collected in this volume are based on the author's publications, as indicated below. The courtesy and the permission of the corresponding editors and publishers are gratefully acknowledged.

"The Royal Yoga" is based on "Yoga: The Royal Path to Freedom" in *Hindu Spirituality: Vedas through Vedanta*. ed. K. Sivaraman (New York: Crossroad Publishers, 1989). Vol. 6 of *World Spirituality: An Encyclopedic History of the Religious Quest.*

"The Dimensions of the Self: *Buddhi* in the Bhagavad Gita" is excerpted from an article with A. Hilary Armstrong in *Religious Studies* 15 (1979) : 317–332.

"Is Religion Psychotherapy?" is based on an article in *Religious Studies* 14 (1978) : 389–397.

"Ahimsa, Transformation and Ecology" is based on an article with the same title published in *Re-Vision: Journal of Consciousness and Transformation* 17 (1995) : 23-29.

"The Yoga of the Cross" is excerpted from *The Gospel of John in the Light of Indian Mysticism* (Rochester, VT: InnerTraditions, 2004).

"The Mill and the Mill-Pond: The Silent Mind of a Yogi" is based on an essay in *Krishnamurti: Two Birds on One Tree* (Wheaton, IL: Quest Books, 1995).

"Gurdjieff Work and the Teaching of Krishna" is from *Gurdjieff: Essays and Reflections on the Man and his Teaching*, ed. J. Needleman and G. Baker (New York: Continuum, 1996) 214–224.

From the Editor

Yoga is now very popular in the West, and yoga centers can be found in almost every town in North America and Europe. Students who find the practice of yoga useful may discover a deepening interest in the possibility that is opened through yoga and a corresponding wish to learn about the roots of yoga and the culture from which it arose. The effect of a yoga practice often leads to the wish to know of the metaphysical and spiritual aspects of the great tradition of its origin. This collection of articles by Ravi Ravindra will be valuable for those who have this wish.

Ravi Ravindra was born in India, where he received his early scientific and metaphysical education. Since then he has spent several decades in the Western world teaching physics, philosophy, and comparative religion. He is particularly suited to the task of introducing us to the spiritual roots of yoga. Ravindra is at home in the East and in the West; he understands hymns in Vedic Sanskrit and nuances of relativistic cosmology, and he brings insights from both sources. He has been deeply influenced by the two great texts of yoga in India—the Bhagavad Gita, in which the God incarnate, Krishna, expounds his yoga to his beloved disciple, Arjuna; and the *Yoga Sutra* attributed to Patañjali. Ravindra also brings insights from other great spiritual traditions in which he has had an abiding interest. He has practiced yoga for many years and has had a longstanding engagement with spiritual search. He brings a passionate inquiry about the meaning and purpose of human life and of the cosmos and exhibits a remarkable impartiality that searches for and delights in truth and wisdom wherever they can be found, without an argument for or an exclusive interest in any sect, religion, or tradition.

Each of the articles here is informed by the philosophical background of yoga. All of them speak of and are related to the wisdom of the spiritual traditions of India. They range from an exploration of *rita* (cosmic order) in the Rig Veda and its relation to *yajña* (sacrifice and exchange between levels) and *dharma* (law, order, sacred obligation) to reflections about contemporary spiritual masters such as J. Krishnamurti and G. I. Gurdjieff, in the context of the Indian tradition. Some of the essays deal exclusively with the great texts of India, whereas some deal with parallels in texts from other traditions, such as the Gospel According to Saint John.

The spirit displayed in these essays is expressed in two remarks that Ravindra often quotes. One, a statement of Jesus Christ:

> *Believe me ... an hour is coming when you will worship the Father neither on this mountain, nor in Jerusalem. An hour is coming, and is already here, when those who are real worshipers will worship the Father in Spirit and in truth. Indeed it is just such worshipers the Father seeks. God is Spirit and those who worship Him must worship in Spirit and in truth (John 4:21, 23–24).*

The other is from the Indian tradition:

> *Koham kathamidam cheti saṁsāramalamātatam*
> *pravichāryam prayatnena prājñena sahasādhunā*
>
> *Who am I? Whence is this widespread cosmic flux?*
> *These, the wise should inquire into diligently,*
> *Soon—nay, now.*
>
> *—Mahopanishad IV, 21*

Some of the essays here have been revised from the original form in which they were published in a variety of journals and books, and in an earlier collection, *Yoga and the Teaching of Krishna*. An attentive reading will reveal a breadth of vision and a depth of understanding expressed with clarity and simplicity. The level of thought and feeling in these reflections invites a response from *buddhi*, the faculty of integrated intelligence, and allows us to share in the movement "from insight to insight," as is said in the Upanishads.

Priscilla Murray, Ph.D.

Introduction

In recent years there has been an increasing interest in yoga throughout the world. In every city and in most small communities in the West, it is possible to find classes in yoga that promote relaxation, physical well-being, and breathing exercises. The word 'yoga' is now used almost universally to refer to the practice of *hatha yoga*, which emphasizes body postures (*asanas*) and develops flexibility. Hatha yoga is only one aspect of yoga, which in its fullness is concerned with the right relationship with the whole of the cosmos. However, even a little of hatha yoga can open a gateway to the larger spiritual tradition. Since body and mind are intimately connected, physical flexibility contributes to an increasing freedom from a rigidity of the mind, which is at the base of all forms of fundamentalism.

Yoga is primordial. It has existed whenever and wherever human beings have attempted to be connected with the All or the One. The longing for, the search for, and the realization of this essential oneness is yoga. As Krishna in the Bhagavad Gita, a text of yoga par excellence, puts it, "A person whose self is integrated by yoga sees the Self in all beings and all beings in the Self, seeing all impartially. Such a yogi, established in oneness and in love for Me, who am present in all beings, living and acting in any manner whatsoever, lives and acts in Me" (BG 6:29, 31).

But yoga is also always modern and relevant. Whenever there are signs of awakening to a need for an integration of body, mind, and heart, there is a need for yoga. This need is felt even more strongly when there is more of an inner fragmentation resulting from a self-centered life-style of competitiveness and domination. An integration of all our parts is essential before a connection with something higher can take place. Only a centered self has the possibility of being selfless and of being centered in the Self.

Even though it is often associated with India, yoga is trans-cultural, almost by definition, for the simple reason that a search for an integrated self is universal. All the great sages everywhere have stressed the importance of the transformation of our ego-self, with its occupation with 'I like it' or 'I don't like it', and with fear and self-importance—the whole domain of 'I-me-mine'—into a self able to be established in the real. Such a transformation is the aim of all spiritual disciplines.

All religions maintain that in general human beings do not live the way they should and, furthermore, the way they could. The expressions and metaphors vary, but the essential point remains—we live in sin but we could live in the grace of God, or we live in sorrow but we could live in the felicity of nirvana, or we live in illusion but we could live in reality. As we ordinarily are, we cannot come to the real. A radical transformation of our whole being is needed, an awakening to a new consciousness, a new birth—spiritual, virginal, not according to our carnal will. Although the need for a radical transformation of being is universal, yoga, a tool for this transformation, has been extensively developed and elaborated in the various spiritual teachings in India.

The theory and the practice of yoga is not something that has been forged or devised from below, or that can even be understood by the human mind, however intelligent such a mind may be. Yoga originates from above, that is to say, from the vision of the highest possible state of consciousness. It is a suprahuman revelation, from the realm of the gods. Speaking mythologically, it is said that the great God Shiva taught yoga to his beloved Parvati for the sake of humanity. It cannot be validated or refuted by human reasoning; on the contrary, the relative sanity or health of a mind is measured by the extent to which it accords with the sayings of the accomplished sages, who have been transformed by the practice of yoga. It is a vision from the third eye, compared with which our two usual eyes see only shadows.

In spite of the revelatory nature of yoga, it is not primarily a matter of faith, and it is not opposed to knowledge. What it in fact requires is the utmost exertion of the whole of the human being—mind, heart, and body—for a practice that leads to a total transformation of being, a change not less than that of a species mutation. Thus, yoga not only brings the vision from the third eye of Shiva for us to receive but also aims at helping us develop and open the third eye in ourselves so that we may be of like spiritual vision with Shiva. This is conveyed by the etymology of the word 'yoga': it is derived from the root yuj, meaning to yoke, unite, harness. When the human body-mind is harnessed to the Spirit, which is as much within a human being as outside, the person is in yoga. The meaning of the word 'yoga' is related to that of 'religion' which is derived from the Latin 'ligare' meaning 'to bind' or 'to connect'. Making or discovering a connection with the Spirit is the aim of yoga, as it is of all true religion.

Yoga refers to the union with a higher, subtler reality as well as to the way or the path to that state of being which is more integrated and is oriented to such a reality. Yoga is at once religion, science, and art, as it is concerned with being, knowing, as well as doing. The aim of yoga, however, is beyond these three, as well as beyond any opposites that they imply. Yoga aims at *moksha*, which is unconditioned and uncaused freedom. This state of freedom is, by its very nature, beyond the dualities of being-nonbeing, knowledge-ignorance, and action-nonaction. The way to moksha is yoga, which serves as a path or a discipline toward integration.

Achieving the aim of yoga requires the transformation of a human being from a natural and actual form to a perfect and real form. In our usual state of being, we act compulsively in reaction to natural forces and tendencies, active both outside and inside us. Ordinarily, we are slaves of the mechanical forces of nature and all our actions are determined by the law of karma, the law of conditioning, and the corresponding action and reaction. Through yoga, however, one can be transformed so that we are no longer wholly at the mercy of unconscious forces and inclinations.

The procedure of yoga corresponds to the root meaning of the word 'education': it helps draw out what in fact already is in us but is not perceivable in the unrefined form. The progressive bringing out of the real person is much like the releasing of a figure from an unshaped stone. The undertaking of yoga concerns the entire person, resulting in a reshaping of mind, body, and emotions; in short, in a new birth. The remolding involved in yoga is essentially from the inside out, and the yogi is the artist, the stone, and the tools. But a person does not create the state of freedom; if one is properly prepared and does not insist on possessing and controlling everything, one can allow what is deep within to surface and express itself.

The analogy between yoga and sculpting should not be misunderstood as suggesting that yoga leads to a rugged individualism in which individuals are the makers of their own destiny. The freedom a yogi aspires to is less a freedom *for* the self and more a freedom *from* the self. From a strict metaphysical point of view, a yogi cannot be said to be the artist of his or her own life; the real initiative belongs only to Krishna, lodged in the heart of everyone (BG 10:20). Furthermore, "Those who see Me in everything and see everything in Me, are not separated from Me and I am not separated from them" says Krishna (BG 6:30).

Yoga begins from an impartial recognition of our human situation. Self-knowledge is both the essential method and goal of yoga. However, self-knowledge is a relative matter. It depends not only on the depth and clarity of insight but also on what is seen as the *self* to be known. A progressive change from the identification of the self as the body (including the heart and the mind) to the identification of the self as inhabiting the body is a crucial development in yoga. Ancient and modern Indian languages reflect this perspective in the expressions they use to describe a person's death: in contrast to the usual English expression of "giving up the ghost," one "gives up the body." It is not the body that has the spirit, but the spirit that has the body. The yogi identifies the person less with the body and more with the embodied.

The identification of the person with something other than the body-mind, and the attendant freedom from the body-mind, is possible only through a proper functioning and restructuring of the body and the mind. The Sanskrit word '*sharira*' is useful in order to steer clear of the modern Western philosophic dilemma called the mind-body problem. Although 'sharira' is usually translated as 'body', it means the whole psychosomatic complex of body, mind, and heart. 'Sharira' has the same import as 'flesh' in the Gospel of John, for example in John 1.14, where it is said, "The Word became flesh and dwelt in us" (for a detailed discussion see Ravindra, *The Gospel of John in the Light of Indian Mysticism*). The important point, both in the Indian context and in John, is that the spiritual element, called *Purusha*, *Atman*, or *Logos* (Word), is above the whole of the psychosomatic complex of a human being, and is not to be identified with mind, which is a part of sharira or the flesh.

Sharira is both the instrument of transformation and the mirror indicating it. The way a person sits, walks, feels, and thinks can lead to a deeper self; the contact with the deeper self is then reflected in the way a person sits, walks, feels, and thinks. Sharira, which is miniaturized or individualized *prakriti* (nature), is the medium necessary for the completion and manifestation of the inner spiritual being, which itself can be understood as individualized *Brahman* (the Vastness), whose body is the whole of the cosmos, subtle as well as gross.

There is a correspondence between the microcosmos, which is a human being, and the macrocosmos or universe. The more developed a person is, the more that person corresponds to the deeper and subtler aspects of the cosmos. Only a fully developed human being mirrors the entire creation. To view sharira or the world as a hindrance rather than an opportunity is akin to regarding the rough stone as an obstruction to the finished sculpture. Sharira is the substance from which each one of us makes a work of art, according to our ability to respond to the inner urge and initiative. This substance includes what are ordinarily called psychic, organic, and inorganic materials. Prakriti, although following strict causality, is alive and purposeful, and every existence, even a stone, has a psyche and purpose. From a traditional perspective, creation is understood to be from above downward—in contrast to the view of modern scientific cosmology that matter precedes mind.

Although there are many kinds of yogas—such as *karma* yoga (integration through action), *bhakti* yoga (union through love), *jñana* yoga (path of knowledge), and others—the Indian tradition has in general maintained that there is only one central yoga, with one central aim of harnessing the entire body-mind to the purposes of the Spirit. Different yogas arise because of the varying emphases on methods and procedures adopted by different teachers and schools. All the yogas, to the extent that they are true, aim at the same thing: to lead the practitioners to an insight naturally full of truth and order (*Yoga Sutra* 1:48) in which one sees that "all there is is Krishna" (BG 7:19), and acts accordingly with compassion and responsibility for the maintenance of the world.

Religion and Yoga

Is Religion Psychotherapy?

"Is religion psychology?" "Is religion physiology?" and "Is religion physiotherapy?" are questions which are related to the question raised in the title. The answer to any of the four questions above is both "yes" and "no." I propose to explore how we might understand these questions in the light of the Bhagavad Gita and Patañjali's *Yoga Sutra*, along with some reference to other sources, but these two texts are of paramount importance in Indian religion and psychology and may be considered representative of the classical Indian view.

Religion as Yoga

The central concern of the Bhagavad Gita and the *Yoga Sutra* is liberation, which for our purposes here describes the point of religion. In order not to become sidetracked by contemporary discussions about the meaning and goal of religion, and whether the word is appropriate or useful to designate what goes on under this label, let me suggest that we use the Sanskrit word 'yoga' for two reasons. The first reason is simply that there is no other Sanskrit word which is more suitable than 'yoga' for translating 'religion'. '*Dharma*' is often translated as 'religion', but it is more appropriately translated as 'duty', 'law', or 'order'. Second, 'yoga' and 'religion' have some close parallels in their etymologies, which refer to a uniting or making a bond between what is human and what is divine, as well as in their explicit associations with diligence, attention, and heedfulness. The importance of yoga in the Indian tradition cannot be exaggerated. A name or an epithet of Shiva is *Yoganatha;* of Vishnu, *Yogapati;* and of Krishna, *Yogeshvara*—which in each case means master or lord of yoga.

One advantage of using 'yoga' rather than 'religion' is the fact that 'yoga' has an associated verb form. In the Bhagavad Gita, for example, the verb form of 'yoga' is used more frequently than the noun form. The word 'religion' does not have a corresponding verb form; this leads to expressions like 'having religion' rather than 'practicing religion'. An expression like 'having yoga' would sound quite odd because yoga is closer to a process than to a doctrine.

Mythologically, Yoga is sometimes personified as the son of Dharma and Kriya; Dharma is essentially the order that is the support of the cosmos, and Kriya, as action and performance, is a *shakti* (energy, power) of Vishnu in his Vamana (dwarf) incarnation. Yoga is science and art as well as religion, since it is concerned with knowing (*jñana*), doing (*karma*) and being (*sat*). The aim of yoga, however, in both the Bhagavad Gita and the *Yoga Sutra*, is beyond these three, as well as beyond any opposites they imply. The state of moksha, that is, of uncaused freedom, which is Krishna's own state (*bhava*), is beyond the dualities of being-non-being, knowledge-ignorance, and activity-inactivity and beyond any opposition or contradiction. The way to moksha is yoga, which is religion as a path and a discipline toward integration.

The Method and Aim of Yoga

The aim of yoga is the transformation of human beings from their natural form to a perfected form. The *prakrita* (literally: natural, vulgar, unrefined) state is one in which a person compulsively repeats actions, in reaction to the forces of prakriti, which are active both outside and inside. Through yoga a person can become *sanskrita* (literally: well made, well put together) and thus no longer be wholly at the mercy of natural forces and inclinations. The procedure of yoga corresponds to the root meaning of 'education', for it helps bring out what is already in a person but which was not perceivable in the unpolished form. The progressive bringing out of Brahman in an aspirant is much like the releasing of a figure from an unshaped stone.

The undertaking of yoga concerns the entire person, resulting in a reshaping of mind, body, and emotions. *Sharira*, which is miniaturized or individualized Prakriti, is the medium necessary for the completion and manifestation of *svabhava*, the inner being which is said to be a particle of Brahman, whose body is the whole manifested cosmos. Each one of us, every existence movable or immovable according to the Bhagavad Gita, comes into being by the union of Prakriti and *Purusha*, or sharira and *Atman*, or the field and the knower of the field. Shiva and Shakti in an intimate embrace symbolize this union resulting in creation. Iconographically, this symbol is further abstracted into Shivalingam (the phallus of Shiva), which is viewed in intercourse from inside the cosmic womb, where each of us comes into being. Each being is from seed placed in the womb of Prakriti by Shiva.

Following the Bhagavad Gita (15.16), we can say this in another way. Each person is made up of three beings: the perishable purusha, the imperishable purusha, and the highest Purusha. The first two are said to be basically different from each other. Although the path of yoga aims at a realization of the fundamental essential unity of all there is, an intermediate stage is one of recognizing the radical duality between the perishable purusha and the imperishable purusha. A yogi sees that part of the self which is independent of sharira, and thus independent of prakriti according to whose laws the body-mind functions. When a yogi has identified the self with the imperishable purusha within, only then can a move be made toward the yet more basic unity of the highest Purusha, where all dualities—metaphysical, ethical, or linguistic—are reconciled. In this state, the perfected yogi, the completely integrated person, sees everything in the Self and the Self in everything. This Self is not personal; it is not one's own, nor another's. This Self (Atman) is what the Upanishads speak of as being identical with Brahman. Nor can one think of this Self as being inside a person and not outside. The Katha Upanishad (11.1:10) says, "What is within us is also without. What is without is also within. He who sees differences between what is within and what is without goes evermore from death to death."

In the Bhagavad Gita, when Arjuna realizes he will be at war with his cousins, with his own teachers, and that some of them will be killed, he loses heart and decides that he will not fight. Krishna, his charioteer, tells Arjuna that he cannot not act, and responds to Arjuna's question not by telling him how to act but by speaking of the Self, the level of reality which is not subject to the processes of time, to birth, death, and change, but which pervades everything. The beginning of Krishna's teaching in the Bhagavad Gita distinguishes between what is natural and in time and what is eternal and beyond time.

Although every way of speaking has limitations and betrays the truth, it might be said that human beings live in two worlds: the world of time and the world of the eternal, or that human beings are subject to two major forces or tendencies: one is the downward force of their lower nature which manifests as desires, inclinations, likes, and dislikes; the other is the upward force of their higher nature which determines their calling. A person's essential being (svạbhava) is the lord seated in the heart which makes each one revolve as if mounted on a machine (BG 18.60). Human beings are advised to follow their *svadharma,* which is the law (or demand or vocation) that corresponds to their svabhava. The work done in accordance with this law is *svakarma.* This work must not be abandoned and cannot be abandoned without violating the most essential part of oneself. Each person is born, incarnated in a specific form at a certain time and place, in response to their previous karma, in order to pursue the dictates of svabhava. The svabhava of human beings in general corresponds to *brahmins* (scholars, teachers, seekers), *kshatriyas* (warriors, administrators, rulers), *vaishyas* (businessmen, artisans, producers), or *shudras* (proletariat, laborers). One can be in the mode (*guna*) of *satva* (clarity, purity, attentiveness), or of *rajas* (passion, activity, egoism), or of *tamas* (sloth, passivity, heedlessness) in any of these divisions. Thus the four svabhavas and the three gunas constitute twelve types of human beings. However, an understanding of the variety of psychological and physical types and their inclinations became the expression of a rigid caste system which does not promote a discovery of svabhava.

Human beings are enjoined to persist in their own svabhava and the corresponding svadharma and to undertake an upward, qualitative transformation in the gunas from tamas to satva. Svabhava determines a person's calling, the guna predominant in life indicates the quality of response. The spiritual principle in a human being takes on a body for the purpose of perfection. As long as it is unfulfilled, it will continue to incarnate itself, setting aside the body-mind when it becomes unsuitable for its purpose. Svabhava, however, is not an end in itself. It is a means by which one can come to share Krishna's bhava. If one is in Krishna's bhava, then one is truly a microcosm mirroring the macrocosm and one acts as Krishna does—in complete freedom, for the sake of sustaining the world order, according to the principle of sacrifice (*yajña*) which maintains the cosmic processes through a reciprocal exchange (BG 3.9). The entire movement of yoga consists of the transformation in which the center of gravity and initiative change from lower nature, with the inclinations and desires of sharira, through higher nature and the call of svabhava, to Krishna's nature or state of Brahman. Krishna identifies himself in the Bhagavad Gita with the supreme Brahman, supreme Atman, and supreme Purusha at different places. He frequently shifts from a personal mode of speaking to an impersonal one. Personal-impersonal, subjective-objective, internal-external, and other such dichotomies are often said to be transcended by the sages.

Yoga as Physiology-Psychology

Sharira, the body-mind, is the field, and Atman (or Purusha) is the knower of the field. Krishna says that true knowledge consists in knowing both the field and the knower of the field (BG 13.2). The knowledge of the field, of the body-mind and the modes of prakriti, or physics in the broadest sense of the word, is a necessary component of yoga. As yoga proceeds by focusing on the internal manifestation of nature, rather than the external, one may prefer to use the word psychology in this context rather than physics or physiology. We should remember, of course, that in the point of view under consideration, psychology and physiology are two sides of the same coin, for a strict correspondence exists between the internal and external forces and materials. Furthermore, given the fact that sharira is both body and psyche, one might equally well have replaced 'psychology' by 'physiology', using these terms in their widest connotations.

Just as the appearance of an unformed stone is different from that of the figure chiseled from it, the psychology or physiology of an ordinary, unformed, prakrita person is not the same as that of an educated, sanskrita person. Yoga psychology begins from where one is, but the description and explanation of ordinary human behavior is only a beginning. The real interest is in the possibility of perfecting human beings. The concern in yoga is not only the diagnosis of the human condition but also the prescription and the effecting of a cure that will make a person whole. The healing of the body-mind is an integral part of yoga. Yoga is thus not only physio-psychology but also physio-psychotherapy.

It is perhaps necessary to remark that yoga physio-psychotherapy aims at a level of being which is quite rare and unusual. Curing subnormally functioning human beings and helping them to live normally is obviously necessary and desirable, but it is not the primary concern of yoga. The healing in yoga is not personal. It is not personal neurosis or defect that yoga wishes to cure; it is the human condition that is of interest. Each one is heir to 'malady' by the mere fact of being human or, to speak more correctly, by the mere fact of being an existent. No doubt, this condition is expressed in a particular form, and therefore may need particular remedies. Thus at any given moment the yoga prescribed for one person is not necessarily the same as that prescribed for another. Nevertheless, the forces being harnessed in yoga are not exclusive to anyone.

One does not struggle against these large forces single-handedly or with only one's own power. The upward force also is more than personal. We, human beings, are between these large forces; we come into existence owing to the interplay of these forces and we are constantly subject to them. An image not uncommon in Indian literature is of two shores: human life is the river that connects the two shores. Both shores are needed for a human existence to have a definite form. The Bhagavad Gita speaks of two major tendencies, the *daivic* and *asuric*, godly and demonic, or upward and downward. Both make demands and create compulsions. Given the thoroughly value-laden, hierarchic system of yoga, we should recognize one demand as 'calling' and the other as 'temptation'. Human beings are between these two currents; their only choice seems to be to align themselves either with the one or with the other, remembering what Jesus Christ said: 'He that is not with me is against me; and he that gathereth not with me scattereth abroad' (Matthew 12:30). The remark of St. Paul (Ephesians 6:12) that we wrestle not against flesh and blood but against principalities, powers, rulers of the darkness of this world, and spiritual wickedness in high places, is apt in this connection, in spite of the different idiom.

Yoga thus attempts to reverse the usual, natural order; it is a struggle against the mechancial pull of the lower aspects of prakriti. In the right and proper order, the initiative and movement are from above: the lower parts of human beings listen to and obey the higher parts. Sharira should do what Purusha (or Atman) demands. Otherwise, from a metaphysical perspective, there will be no point to the present incarnation. The body-mind is animated in order to serve the demands of the inner being. If a person is ill-prepared and unable to hear the call or to respond, then sharira has no meaning and no purpose, except as a function of the natural processes. From the point of view of Purusha, this incarnation would then have been wasted in an unsuccessful experiment or it will have been a mistake. A properly educated person, in response to the inner call of Purusha, does what needs to be done, without undue concern for comfort or discomfort. At the end of the Bhagavad Gita (18.73), when Arjuna says to Krishna "I will do thy bidding", the informed sharira willingly offers itself as an instrument for the purposes of the highest Purusha.

Within sharira there exists a hierarchy of organs and functions. More or less adherence to the right internal order indicates the degree of preparation of the sharira, the temple, vehicle, and the instrument of the inner principle. The ordinary mind (*manas*) can follow the desires of the senses, as is the usual case, or it can be receptive to the initiative of *buddhi* (higher mind-heart, intelligent will, integrated intelligence) and direct the senses. Only in the latter case can the call of Purusha be heard, for buddhi alone is capable of this subtle hearing and seeing. If manas and the senses are not guided by buddhi, they cannot be useful to Purusha. *Chitta* (mental consciousness) includes not only reason but also emotions. The lower emotions, unlike the higher ones proper to buddhi such as *bhakti* (love and devotion) and *shraddha* (faith), arise from *samkalpa*, which is imagination or desire-will, and are nourished by sensual pleasure and displeasure.

The first five steps, out of a total of eight, in the *Yoga Sutra* are intended to bring the senses and the other vital functions, in particular the breath, under a conscious control of buddhi. The quality of breathing in a person is intimately and directly connected with the inner state, as is apparent from even a superficial observation of oneself. Traditional appreciation of this fact is reflected in words like *pneuma,* which in Greek means 'breath' and 'air' as well as 'spirit', or Atman, which in Sanskrit means 'self' or 'spirit' and also means 'breath', like its German cognate '*atmen*'. The first two steps aim at a general ethical and attitudinal preparation for undertaking yoga. The next three steps concentrate on posture, breath, and an inward turning of all the senses. Assuming at this stage a certain quietening of the senses, the last three steps of yoga attempt to bring chitta under the subjection of that which is higher.

The various steps of yoga are ordered yet are not sequentially linear in the sense that a completion of one step is required before the next one can be undertaken. Some of the apparent linearity arises from an analytical and linguistic exposition. The earlier steps are preparatory to the later ones, but do not determine them completely. A right physical posture or moral conduct may aid inner development but it does not guarantee it; more often, the external behavior reflects the inner development. For example, a person does not necessarily become wise by breathing or thinking in a particular way; but breathes and thinks in a certain way because of the level of wisdom.

Although moral, physical, and mental cultures are important components of yoga, the point of the effort is beyond the body-mind. The aim of yoga is transcendent. The whole of the physio-psychological work is a preparation of the vehicle to make it fit and suitable for the descent of the spirit. However, none of this work can coerce the spirit. There is no knowledge or method by which we can appropriate the spirit; the only thing we can do is to prepare ourselves so that we may be appropriated by the spirit[1]. But the spirit needs a suitable place. It is well recognized in Indian lore that when spiritual experiences occur without a proper preparation of the body and the mind, the tremendous forces involved can shock the organism into severe illness or insanity. There is a legend about sage Bhagiratha who performed austerities for the descent to the earth of the sacred Ganga, the river which flows in heaven. It was feared that the earth could not bear the shock of her fall. Shiva, the lord of yogis and dancers, caught Ganga on his head and checked her course with his matted locks, and then she flowed from there in seven streams. This is why he is called Gangadhara, upholder of the Ganga. Microcosmically, for the stream of wisdom to descend without destruction, one would need the strength of Shiva riding his bull Nandi, having burnt Kama, the god of desire, with his third eye, and being able to drink the poison which would have resulted in the destruction of the world.

The most significant aspect of yoga and the one which distinguishes it from ordinary physio-psychotherapy, is the transcendent nature of its aim. That which yogis seek does not serve their own purposes. In fact, as long as we have our own purposes, we cannot be really open to higher purposes. The whole meaning of religious life can be understood as a progressive freedom from the hindrances that impede our availability to the purposes of the suprapersonal intelligence.

Yoga physiology or psychology takes its direction and significance from the reality which is beyond the body or the psyche. This renders the physio-psychology of yoga sacred. The cultivation of the body or the mind for their own sake is not yoga. Physical and mental gymnastics performed for material rewards or at best for the pleasures of the body or the mind in the sports world and academia remain at the physical and the psychological level. This is not a condemnation of the very great achievements in these areas, but they do not lead to moksha. Normal physical and psychological functioning is necessary but not sufficient. Perhaps the major cause of our contemporary cultural disorientation is the lack of connection between scholarly, artistic, and scientific research and search for the transcendent. This shortcoming exists not only in practice but even in the prevailing theory of knowledge. Without a movement along the vertical spiritual axis, any adjustment in the psyche constitutes only a horizontal rearrangement of more subtle matter. To confuse these two dimensions is a mistake, to ignore the horizontal dimension is dangerous, and to forget the vertical dimension leads to illusion and bondage.

1 *This point radically distinguishes modern Western science, with its external approach and urge to control what it studies, from ancient sciences, Eastern or Western, dedicated to the harmonization and conciliation of the knower and the object of knowledge.*

Modernization, Westernization and Secularization in India

> WE, THE PEOPLE OF INDIA, having solemnly
> resolved to constitute India into a SOVEREIGN,
> SECULAR, SOCIALISTIC DEMOCRATIC
> REPUBLIC and to secure to all its citizens:
> JUSTICE, social, economic and political;
> LIBERTY of thought, expression, belief, faith
> and worship;
> EQUALITY of status and of opportunity; and to
> promote among them all
> FRATERNITY assuring the dignity of the
> individual and the unity of the Nation
> IN OUR CONSTITUENT ASSEMBLY this
> twenty-sixth day of November 1949, do HEREBY
> ADOPT, ENACT AND GIVE TO OURSELVES
> THIS CONSTITUTION.

Thus reads the preamble to the Constitution of Modern India adopted as India gained its independence from British rule. The two words 'secular' and 'socialistic' were added, by a special constitutional amendment, during the emergency imposed in India during 1975–1977.

In India, modernization still primarily means Westernization, not only in socio-political institutions but also quite comprehensively. India seems to aspire toward Western modes of thought in education, research, and management, and toward industrialization according to the procedures and developments of Western science and technology, Western social values and goals, and Western institutions of government, information, and warfare. No doubt all of these institutions, procedures, and modes of thought are quite modern within the Western world. But they show discernible continuities with earlier Western sensibilities and practices. Arising out of the Western soil, they are likely to be more in tune with the Western soul. However, either owing to military and economic pressures or because of the seduction of progress and success, these modern Western values and aspirations have been adopted by the whole world. Thus, although modernization is a universal phenomenon, leading to some global promises and problems, in the non-Western world it still has a peculiarly alien flavor and external character.

From India's point of view, the initiative for any change or innovation has been outside her borders and control more than two hundred years, until quite recently. What is true for India is, of course, true for what Westerners and, following them now, most Indians, call Hinduism; for Hinduism without India is an abstraction, as is India without Hinduism.

Something needs to be said about Hinduism and the reason for my unease regarding this word. I am not clear what Hinduism is. Even the label 'Hindu' is quite problematic. Until fairly recently it seems to have been a synonym for 'Indian'. These days a 'Hindu' is often understood by exclusion to mean 'an Indian who is not a Muslim nor a Christian.' The word 'Hinduism' seems to suggest, at the very least, that it is a 'religion'. When I try to translate 'religion' into Hindi or Sanskrit, I cannot find any exact translation, but an appropriate word for 'religion' may be 'yoga', as it was discussed in the previous chapter. This is so at least to the extent that we might assume that the Bhagavad Gita and Patañjali's *Yoga Sutra* have something to do with what is meant by religion, since their central concern is *moksha* or liberation. Even the etymologies of 'yoga' and 'religion' have some close parallels in terms of making a bond between what is human and what is divine, as well as in their explicit associations with diligence and attention.

We might well use expressions like 'Hinduyoga' and 'Christianyoga' for what we now label as 'Hinduism' and 'Christianity'. From a Hindu point of view, relatively more specific expressions would be even more appropriate for different aspects within these traditions, like 'the yoga of Katha Upanishad' or 'the yoga of *Theologia Germanica*'; or a set of expressions like 'mantra yoga', 'karma yoga', and 'yoga of the prayer of the heart'. If these expressions were widely used in connection with various religions and their developments, many of the apparently peculiar characteristics of Hinduism would not appear so strange after all. For example, one would not feel odd in being a Hindu and a Christian simultaneously; certainly no more than in following karma yoga and jñana yoga at the same time. No easy eclecticism is advocated here. I am simply drawing attention to an obvious point, almost universally forgotten in practice, that our conceptual apparatus tries to cast all reality in its own mold. What appears strange to us may, from another *darshana* or perspective, seem quite normal. The chief value of comparative studies may lie precisely in their ability to make us aware of our presuppositions.

Another word that is sometimes used to render 'religion' into Sanskrit is 'dharma'. Dharma has in it the connotations of order, law, responsibility, obligation, duty, and righteousness. No being is exempt from the workings and demands of dharma. Every aggregate of the constituents of prakriti, which we can understand to be the agency or the force responsible for making anything that can be an object, whether gross like a stone or subtle like thoughts or feelings, is subject to laws. But no manifestation whatsoever is wholly an object. Every existence has a self, which partakes of the Self, and therefore has obligations in the general maintenance of the cosmic order. This interplay of order, law, and obligation is what determines dharma for any creature. Thus, we act in accord with dharma if we respond to the obligations laid upon us by right order, as we understand it according to our capacity. Bees, snakes, trees, and stars all act in accordance with their dharma, perhaps without a conscious understanding and without complication. The dharma of a human being in any given situation is not easy to be sure about, as is amply illustrated by the complexities in the vast Mahabharata, and may require immense subtlety of thought and feeling to be understood. But Hindus seem to revel in these complexities, and none of their myths, philosophies, arts, or literature are ever simple or straightforward. Since several large forces—cosmic, planetary, social, and individual—make their demands simultaneously on a human being, each according to its own law, a precise understanding of a person's responsibilities in a given situation requires discernment, dedication, and effort.

This point is dramatically brought out and elaborated in the Bhagavad Gita. From the very first word in this remarkable text, the whole dialogue, as Krishna himself says toward the end (BG 18.70), is about dharma. The root meaning of 'dharma' in the Bhagavad Gita is much the same as it is in the Rig Veda, the earliest work known to India, and also as in the writings of Sri Aurobindo in our own time, namely, the upholding of the orderly relatedness of all that is. In this tradition, which has been continuous for at least five thousand years, dharma is said to be eternal (*sanatana*), since it is based on truths that are timeless and therefore valid for all time, although no doubt our interpretation of them and response to them may vary in time. Sanatana dharma is not made by any person or by any god; it is prior to them. It is the support of the entire creation; it is the ordering principle of all that exists; it is the first and the highest principle of manifestation. There are tendencies and forces that aid the maintenance of dharma and there are others that oppose it. The whole cosmic drama is played out between these two large currents; one may choose to be in one current or the other, but no one may opt out of the game. No one, that is, who is bound by manifestation (*maya*), gross or subtle. But it is possible for a human being to be free of all specific dharmas, if the individual is able to identify the self completely with the highest purusha (spirit, person). Then that person is bound by nothing. According to the Bhagavad Gita, such a person participates in Krishna's own mode of being, that of unconditioned freedom (moksha). This is the end of human dharma, and the goal of human beings. Yoga provides the means to attain this end.

Dharma has a large community component in it, whereas yoga refers to a more individual search. The contrast can be understood by the examples of marriage and love. Marriage is discussed at length in the *dharmashastras*, but only a yoga, namely the bhakti yoga, corresponds to love. However, we can exaggerate the separation of yoga and dharma a little too much, for they are quite related to each other. Mythologically, sometimes Yoga is personified as the son of Dharma and Kriya (action, performance). From the traditional Hindu point of view, the purpose of any specific dharma is to lead beyond itself. The purpose of the whole manifested cosmos and of all social organizations and of all human activities such as philosophy, ritual, and art is to help every creature realize the identity of its self (Atman) and the great self (*Brahman*). Thus art is not for the sake of art itself; it is, if it serves its function rightly, a way to what is beyond art and beyond manifestation. Similarly, a society functions properly only when it enables its members to engage with concerns that are higher than social. On the individual level, a mind is healthy when it is able to know its proper place and is able to listen to what is above it.

According to the Chandogya Upanishad, when Shvetaketu Aruneya was twelve years old, his father Uddalka asked him to live the life of a student, for no one in their family was unlearned and a brahmin only by birth. He returned at the age of twenty-four, having studied all the sciences, greatly conceited, thinking himself well-read. His father then said to him, "Shvetaketu, since you now are so greatly conceited, think yourself well-read and self-important, did you ask for that instruction by which the unhearable becomes heard, the unperceivable becomes perceived, the unknowable become known?" Shvetaketu wondered, "How, Sir, can there be such a teaching?" The generic name for all such teaching is 'yoga'. A society functioning rightly according to dharma makes yoga possible, but only a society that heeds those who are integrated (*yukta*) can truly know what dharma is and function according to it.

Returning now to 'religion', we can perhaps say that from the point of view of the Hindus it may be more appropriately described in terms of dharma and yoga, neither of which needs to have any exclusivist or sectarian meaning, nor any churchly implications. Also, both dharma and yoga are much more holistic than religion, particularly as the latter has come to be understood in the modern West, where it has become a matter of course to separate religion from philosophy, science, politics, education, and art. Furthermore, and most important, dharma and yoga do not serve any exclusively social ends, nor are they ends in themselves; their whole point is transcendent. In terms of dharma and yoga one cannot even properly raise the question similar to "Is religion socially useful or relevant?" In the Indian context, the question is more: 'Is a given society sufficiently in accord with dharma so that yoga can be practiced for the sake of moksha?"

To the extent that Hinduism means dharma and yoga leading to moksha, it is not really a religion, for all human aspirations and efforts toward transcendence can be so described. And, if it does not mean dharma and yoga leading to moksha, from the point of view of the above metaphysical perspective, Hinduism is quite pointless, whatever it stands for. Perhaps, then, by Hinduism is meant that cluster of understandings and forms of dharma and yoga which had their main inspiration and development in India. I say 'perhaps' because I am not really sure about this, especially because in the vast and ancient culture of India so many different forms and interpretations have emerged that with sufficient ingenuity most major ideas and practices can be discovered there. Given the general Hindu tendency to think that every form, however twisted and perverse it may seem to the majority, derives ultimately from Divine energy and is likely to elevate its sincere devotee, and given a very high level of tolerance among Hindus for conceptual and aesthetic chaos, no form is ever completely eliminated. There is such an exuberant riot of cults, practices, gods, mythologies, philosophies—everything on a stupendous scale—that no one addicted to logical and clear formulations in all spheres of life is likely to find Hinduism satisfactory, manageable, or palatable.

With these hesitations, we can come back to modernization. Moksha is, by definition, not analyzable in terms of any rational categories or any other temporal forms. Although it is the goal of Hinduism, and of any other path in time based on sanatana dharma, moksha refers to a timeless state, not opposed to time but independent of it. Hinduism is not synonymous with sanatana dharma. It is, at best, an instance of sanatana dharma as understood, expressed, and practiced in time and space. Even if the whole of India were to disappear, along with Hinduism, from the surface of the earth, sanatana dharma would still remain. The eternal remains, even if at any given moment it may not have any visible illustration. When Hindus say that all religions are essentially the same, what they are referring to is the transcendental unity of religions, and not to a similarity of religious forms. It is their belief, and for Ramakrishna it was a knowledge, that to the extent that any religion leads to transcendent reality, it is because it is a form of sanatana dharma, which is like a tree with its roots in heaven and with many branches on earth.

Yoga, being a teaching "by which the unhearable becomes heard," is subject to change in time, but only in its beginning stages where the outermost personality of a seeker is predominant and the teacher adapts the teaching to suit the pupil's particular predilections. This outermost personality is what is most affected by social conditioning and therefore by contingencies of history and geography. To the extent that a given yoga is able to lead to truth, it is an instrument that transforms an aspirant from his time-bound outermost self to his time-freed innermost Self. The varieties of yoga, which here means path or teaching for transformation, correspond to the different basic types of human beings and do not essentially change with time in their inner content, although it is true that in any given period of history a particular type of person may be predominant, requiring a corresponding yoga.

Cultural dharma, which constantly changes due to the constant interaction of external and internal forces of innovation and the preserving tendencies of the tradition, is most affected by history. This dharma is subject to rapid change, largely initiated by strong external forces. At the risk of being extremely simplistic, we may choose the traditional metaphor of the wheel: the center, which exists everywhere, indicates moksha; the spokes are the various yogas leading to the center, and the rim is cultural dharma, touching the road of history but drawing its integrity and strength from the center. Moksha is neither personal nor social; nor, of course, nonpersonal or nonsocial. Yoga is personal in the beginning of a spiritual journey, and dharma is social. It is appropriate to say, as the Bhagavad Gita clearly implies, that our individual dharma relates our social dharma and personal yoga. In our metaphor of the wheel, an individual human being is situated at the meeting point of a spoke and the rim. From other points of view, the whole wheel, including the spokes, can be spoken of as representing dharma.

We may now return to the preamble of the constitution of modern India. A constitution that the people of India "give to ourselves" is not regarded as having a transcendent reference. This constitution comes neither from heaven as *shruti* (revelation) heard by the sages, nor from the ancestors as *smriti* (tradition) incorporating the cumulative experience of the community, dependent on sanatana dharma as perceived, understood, and interpreted by the wisest of the society. The constitution is, both in its spirit and origin, entirely Western. "We wanted the music of Veena or Sitar," remarked a member of the Constitution Assembly responsible for approving the draft constitution, "but here we have the music of an English band" (Austin, p. 325). In a reversal of the traditional order, the constitution self-consciously takes its stand on earth and not in heaven. Its fundamental notions of social justice, liberty, and equality were developed in the West, during the period when the center of gravity of that culture was unrelated to, if not in opposition to, transcendent concerns.

Christianity has had a significant effect on India. Many Christian missionaries, more pious than wise, had quite fantastic and absurd impressions about Hinduism, often resulting from their definite, but ignorant, convictions about idols, sexual symbolism, and polytheism. Of course, as was said earlier, it is not easy to remain unconfounded in front of the gargantuan multi-dimensionality of Hinduism in which everything from the most sublime to the most bizarre has its place. Even the venomous serpent Kaliya, who had caused much panic and discomfort to everyone around the place in the Yamuna River where he had lodged himself, on being overpowered by Krishna claimed to have acted in accordance with his snake dharma in spreading his poison around. Krishna found this explanation quite acceptable and spared Kaliya's life, merely banishing him to the ocean, a more appropriate place for the serpent's activities. If one has a simplistic notion about right and wrong, one is likely to be bewildered by all that can go on under the umbrella of Hinduism. Many well-intentioned European Christians were scandalized by Hinduism and made some quite uncharitable and misinformed comments about it.

Here is a remark made by the eminent missionary Reverend Alexander Duff, who lived in India from 1830 to 1863 and who did much to promote education and social reform: "Of all the systems of false religion ever fabricated by the perverse ingenuity of fallen man, Hinduism is surely the most stupendous. ... Of all systems of false religion it is that which seems to embody the largest amount and variety of semblances and counterfeits of divinely revealed facts and doctrines" (Majumdar, part II, p. 155).

In spite of all this, because the above is hardly the whole truth about Christian activities in India, Christianity also contributed to the purification and reform of the Hindu society. All internal reform movements among the Hindus in the last one hundred years or so had their explicit or implicit reference to Christianity, and came into existence in opposition to, in imitation of, or in accommodation with Christianity. Christian scriptures and many Christians dedicated to the care of the sick and the poor sparked the awakening of conscience among the Hindus about the plight of the downtrodden in their own society. Christians, such as Mother Teresa, who have made a difference to so many lives in India, have been respected and admired for their selfless work.

It is difficult to exaggerate either the necessity of social reforms or their desirability. When the understanding and practice of cultural dharma is awry, there is a need to correct it. The constitution also provides a corrective to any tendency to ignore the plight of a large number of citizens of India. Nevertheless, just as Christ's "kingdom is not of this world," social reform even at its best cannot be considered as humanity's highest end. What gives religion significance, from the Hindu point of view, is beyond social good, although it is clearly not opposed to it. Christianity in India did not provide—what in any case would have been an astounding achievement anywhere—a functioning model of active engagement with social welfare along with an emphasis on transcendent concerns. It is difficult to escape the impression that in the modern world, in the West or in the East, Christianity on the large has been basically a social force, which by itself could hardly be undervalued. Its transcendent yearnings have not been able to challenge society about its own raison d'être. Perhaps this is just another way of saying that in modern times, societies that are nominally Christian are basically secular in their aspirations.

Another aspect of modernization and the accompanying secularization needs to be mentioned, namely, science and technology. Yesterday's 'rice Christians' in India are today's 'wheat technologists'. Science has been the major intellectual and social influence in the modern West. Owing to its close relationship with technology, it is a significant factor in military and economic power. And this sort of power is all that matters in the world, unless there is some moral or spiritual power in opposition to it or pushing it in a different direction. Even within the Western world, modern natural science has driven itself like a wedge in the history of thought, creating a deep cleavage in the intellect of humanity. It is a fact of Western intellectual history that every major poet and artist since Newton's founding of natural science on a firm footing has felt uneasy about the assumptions, procedures, or results of the scientific enterprise. However, perhaps because of the separation among the domains of truth, beauty, and goodness that prevails in the mind of the modern Western person, science has moved on, wholly indifferent to these critics, like a large iceberg unaffected by the thrashings of small fish.

Modern science and technology have not arisen and developed in a metaphysical vacuum. There are many cultural values and metaphysical assumptions about the nature and purpose of human beings, about the cosmos, and about knowledge that underlie their development. These assumptions are products of Western European history and philosophy. Modern science and technology, not withstanding the recurring large-scale uneasiness with them, are as Western in character as Western music or sculpture. Western science is as distinct from Indian science, in its fundamental attitude and purpose, as Western harmony is from the Indian *raga*. It is not often remarked that modern natural sciences represent one among many possible ways of approaching nature. This way is no more unique or exclusively God-given than Christianity was claimed to be by its adherents. There are many interesting parallels between contemporary organized science and organized Christianity of the nineteenth and earlier centuries, including the unilateral insistence on being the one true way. 'Pious' practicing scientists cannot even understand that somebody can seriously raise a question about the 'way' of doing science. There can be, and have been, different approaches to the study of nature and human life, informed by different purposes and yielding different results. An example of a branch of science developed in India is yoga, with its quite different base, intention, and consequences, as contrasted with its counterparts in Western science, namely physiology, psychology, and medicine. As we saw earlier, yoga is also religion. However, religion and science are wholly separated in the modern West, and whatever religion may be, it is not considered knowledge. One result of this situation is that modern science is completely divorced from any transcendent concerns, and it has thus been the chief force of secularization in the modern world.

The major problem faced by India now is how to reconcile the demands of time and the demands of what is timeless. Or, in terms of social needs, how to meet the needs of the body as well as of the spirit. This question has a different pathos in India, whose poverty has become as proverbial as her richness used to be. There, among the intelligentsia and among those with some social conscience, where the awareness of the problems and needs of the manifested world is so overwhelming, any concern for the unmanifest reality is beginning to look indecent, immoral, and even insane. An important factor in the situation is the awareness of the presence of Western culture with its immense material prosperity, military might, technical knowledge, and virtual control over most global institutions and resources. The enormous worldly power of the West makes all its cultural styles and practices desirable and worthy of emulation in the eyes of a people who have not had such demonstrable worldly success in recent history. Whether drawn to the liberal democratic style or the Marxist-communist mode, almost everyone among the educated youth in modern India seems to consider social ideals as ultimate, and Western science and technology as the basic means.

Clearly, the needs of the body cannot be denied; a starving person cannot attend to the spirit. The cry of the Earth cannot be ignored. The West has obviously made, and will continue to make, significant contributions to human welfare throughout the world, and not least in India.

Still, if the body of Indian society were to survive and prosper without being at the same time a temple of the spirit, it would be an existence without significance. As long as modernization in India continues to mean primarily Westernization, it is difficult to be sanguine about the possibility of the triumph of the spirit. Not because the West is alien (the time for such parochial sentiment is past in the emerging planetary culture), but because the modern West does not speak with the power of its own spiritual depths. For the sake of the whole planet, India and Hinduism need to grow a new body for their ancient spirit to make a new response to the demands of the earth. The realm of technique and materiality cannot be neglected without the risk of subjugation or starvation. But the very purpose for which one exists, or for which society exists, can be easily forgotten in the midst of social concerns and worldly success. If India ceases to make room for the wild geese (*hamsa*) among human beings, who respond to the call of the other shore, how would the world know the dance of Shiva, the Divine Outsider? The whole herd of starving lions in search of food and security may well be lured into cages, and be tamed to perform worldly tricks, forgetting the jungle-reverberating roar of a free lion like the Buddha. Arjuna, the archer, is needed for the protection of dharma, but he must always submit himself to the purpose of Krishna, the lord of yoga. In the imagery of the Rig Veda, our mother is Earth and our father is Heaven; who among the children will dare to hold Heaven and Earth in a new embrace?

Can Consciousness Survive Birth?

Often, especially in the modern Western cultural context, a question "Can consciousness survive the death of the body?" is raised. I entreat you to consider a question that is raised from another perspective: "Can consciousness survive birth and the life of the body?"

My intention in raising this reverse question is not to be merely perverse or clever or only to play with words. We think and raise questions and expect certain sorts of answers within a framework of rationality in the context of a worldview. Although these worldviews themselves are permeable and elastic at the borders and can change, they are fairly solid in the main and are founded on many tacit assumptions. My intention in rephrasing the question the way I have is to bring to light some of the presuppositions of the contemporary framework within which these questions are usually raised.

In the process I hope to present an alternative point of view, which is an ancient perspective, or, one might say, using traditional language, that it is from the *beginning*, for "In the beginning is the Spirit."

If we were wholly convinced that the stars are held together in their places by the physical attraction of gravitation alone—and it is quite irrelevant whether we understand gravitation according to the Newtonian theory or according to the Theory of General Relativity of Einstein—what sense could we make of the last stanza of Dante's *The Divine Comedy* which speaks of "the love that moves the sun and the other stars?" We could hardly understand the cosmic force of love, which is as much an integral constituent of the highest state of consciousness as delight and wisdom.

A few preliminary remarks are useful, even though they can be made only in a very abbreviated form here. In general, *consciousness* and its various levels and states have been well elaborated in the Hindu-Buddhist traditions. But this does not seem to be the case in the Biblical traditions in general. In the Biblical traditions, the emphasis is more on *conscience* than on *consciousness*. If we examine this matter with critical sympathy, we shall see that this major difference between the Biblical and the Indic traditions—that of emphasis on conscience or on consciousness—is related to another major difference between the two main streams of spirituality. In the Biblical traditions, the root cause of the human predicament is the assertion of self-will as opposed to obedience to the will of God. In the Indic traditions, on the other hand, the root cause of the human difficulty is ignorance, which in its turn gives rise to suffering (*dukkha*) or to illusion (maya). In one case, the submission of our will in obedience to the will of God is needed; in the other case the requirement is for the sword of gnosis (jñana) which will cut the knot of ignorance.

Another related fundamental difference follows from this. In the Indic traditions, to hold on to a separate individuality in any ultimate sense is a mark of ignorance, whereas in the Biblical traditions a lack of individuality—even in the presence of God—is a mark of a lack of responsibility. In one case, the general traditional emphasis is on the *oneness* of all there is, whereas in the other case the emphasis is on the *uniqueness* of human beings from all other creatures and of each person with respect to one another. The words 'oneness' and 'uniqueness' are derived from the same root, but their meanings diverge radically. The traditions that hold the ideal of oneness are insight-oriented and have developed a great deal of wisdom about various levels of consciousness. These levels have always to do with degrees of steadiness of attention and gradations of clarity of perception. The traditions extolling uniqueness are faith- and obedience-oriented and have a great deal to say about individual responsibility and moral conscience, corresponding to the quality of virtuous conduct or the degree and the gravity of sinfulness. Whereas levels of consciousness are emphasized in one case, levels of conscience are stressed in the other. Characteristic illustrations of these remarks can be found in two well-known traditional texts: *The Tibetan Book of the Dead* and Dante's *The Divine Comedy*, both dealing with the journey of the soul after death and both concerned with the cultivation of the right quality of life.

It is possible, but neither generous nor insightful, to convince oneself that half the sages in the world just plain misunderstood the matter and only the other half found the truth. Of course, once certain modes of expression are used in a cultural and linguistic context, a traditional momentum develops. Only those modes and terms seem appropriate to the followers which were used by the great teachers in that tradition. This is not harmful by itself, but the trouble arises when the dogmatic section in any tradition insists that truth can only be expressed in one form. What is much more likely is that in these differences and contradictions—between the emphasis on consciousness rather than on conscience and the other way around—we encounter the difficulties of articulating in a logical and rational language the realities experienced in subtler states of awareness. All the great teachers have said in one form or another that experience of God or Truth or Nirvana or Brahman or the Ultimate cannot be expressed in the language of the lower levels. A radical transformation of conscience-consciousness, a spiritual rebirth, is needed for us to experience the Real. Therefore, it is much more likely that the various sages have articulated significant truths in different ways, often constrained by the abilities of the pupils and the specific language of discourse, emphasizing what they themselves found helpful.

Consciousness, Soul, and Spirit

'Consciousness' is indeed a felicitous word: it allows us to include much of the useful and relevant material that was classically discussed under the rubric of words such as 'mind', 'soul', and 'spirit', without having to be stuck with the religious or philosophical dogmas attached to them. We do not for the present purposes need more precision than is afforded by the word 'consciousness' and its many levels, which refer to the variations among different creatures and within the same person. The important thing is the quality of consciousness which is the quality of awareness. The higher the level of consciousness of a being at a given moment, the more aware such a being is at that time. Consciousness can be completely disorganized and incoherent or it can have a clarity and integrity. It can be at the level of a coarse and heavy materiality or at the level of the angels, who barely leave a footprint or cast a material shadow but whose presence can be felt by sensitive and innocent hearts. Sad is the life of a person who has never experienced, either within the self or in another, a quality of presence that exists without material weight, that acts without a ponderous medium, that cannot be compelled but comes as a sacred benediction, blessing all who are vulnerable to it.

One note of caution needs to be sounded here: we should not fall into the Cartesian dualism of mind and body. Descartes explicitly identified mind with soul and the latter with spirit, all three being radically different from matter or body. For him, and for much of the subsequent philosophy and theology in the West, there has been a duality between the mind and the body, or between the soul and the body, or between spirit and matter. By contrast, the point of view adopted here proceeds from the assumption that there is one energy which permeates the entire cosmos, visible and invisible, gross and subtle, but it manifests at different levels of being and of consciousness. At the highest level pure awareness without materiality exists, and at the lowest level materiality without awareness is present. These limits are like the theoretical limits in mathematics, and are not to be met with in the realm of manifestation, which is the realm of nature. This one energy has been variously called Brahman, *Prana*, *Om*, *Shunyata*, and God. There are schools, for example the Advaita Vedanta, which can be and have been interpreted as saying that the highest level, which is Brahman, is the only one which is real and that all manifestation is maya or illusory. However, it is also possible to understand this as an assertion that all levels are real and sacred because all of them are various manifestations of the same one energy, apart from which nothing exists.

This understanding of one energy needs to be distinguished from an apparently similar idea in modern science. It is an assumption in science that various forms of energy are inter-convertible. The law of conservation of momentum-energy in a closed system presupposes this inter-convertibility. Therefore, from the scientific point of view we could quite rightly speak of one energy pervading the entire cosmos. However, in science, although there are many *forms* of energy, we cannot legitimately speak of many *levels* of energy. The notion of levels, although extremely difficult to pin down rigorously, is crucially important in understanding any of the traditional systems of thought. Imagine making any sense of Dante without some notion of differences in levels! Confining our attention to Indian thought at present, the one energy is manifested at different levels, which have different degrees of consciousness not only quantitatively but also qualitatively. The idea of consciousness is inherent in the notion of levels, and vice versa. Energies—or beings, when we speak theologically or in the mode of persons (God, angels, humans) rather than cosmologically—at a higher level have higher consciousness than those at a lower level. There is a hierarchy in all traditional spiritual thought that is absent in modern science, which confines itself to one horizontal level.

The idea of the unity of spirit and matter includes the unity of consciousness and matter and thus of all nature, for spirit is at the end of the spectrum of One Energy which is totally conscious, whereas matter exists at all other levels, whether we are speaking about only the physical matter or biologically alive organic matter or psychically capable gray matter. It is obvious that spiritual, psychic, as well as biological and physical phenomena exist, even though sometimes prior philosophical commitments make it difficult for people to acknowledge all of these. Also, a relationship between spirit and matter is hardly in question: no spiritual or mental—which is different from spiritual—phenomenon can be studied without some mind and body experiencing it and interacting with it; otherwise we cannot know that such a phenomenon exists. The important question is: Are mind and spirit results of more and more complex organization of matter or do different levels of matter result from differentiation or crystallization (or grossification) of the energy of consciousness? The view that consciousness produces matter is a universal view of spiritual-religious traditions.

Who Am I? Who Are You?

The question of the survival of consciousness after physical death presupposes that it is the body which has consciousness. The assumption that matter precedes mind, intelligence, consciousness, and spirit is a general assumption of modern scientific thought. In that sense, modern science is materialistic: whatever be the difficulties of understanding the origins of matter, the assumption is that in the beginning was matter. To substitute words such as 'energy' or 'spacetime' for 'matter' does not mitigate against the fundamental characteristic of matter in question here, namely, its unconsciousness or lack of awareness or of mindfulness. It is assumed that life at the most rudimentary level comes about by an organization of increasingly complex dead material particles and that further structural organization leads to consciousness or intelligence or spirit. From superheated hadrons, fermions, and the like, electrons, protons, and neutrons arise, which in turn lead to amoeba, which in their turn lead to Einstein with his General Theory of Relativity and the 'cosmic religious feeling' and to Bach with his fugues and his hearing the cherubim and the seraphim singing "Holy, holy, holy!"

This materialist assumption shows clearly that we think that it is the body which has consciousness. Naturally, then, it is a sensible question to ask whether consciousness can survive physical death. If I am the body, and I have enough awareness to know that all creatures die and disappear, I realize that my body will die. Then what will happen to me? Will I still continue living somehow, in some subtle form, with some memories, some form of consciousness? Identifying myself with this body-mind, like the shell of some crustaceans, which others and myself refer to by my name and take photographs of, I have forgotten the real person who inhabits the shell.

What Is the Real Person? Who Am I?

> *Who am I? Whence is this widespread cosmic flux?*
> *These, the wise should inquire into diligently,*
> *soon—nay, now.*
>
> —*Mahopanishad* IV, 21

It is possible to wonder if it is the consciousness which has the body (including the mind). An awakening to the real, to the realization that the person within is one with Brahman or with God, brings a freedom from death, or from death and re-death, the endless cycle of birth and death, as is classically said in India. This is the principle concern of yoga and of spiritual disciplines everywhere.

All spiritual traditions assert, in different ways and with different metaphors, that there is some reason and purpose for the existence of the world and for human beings. The discovery and fulfillment of the purpose for which a human being has been incarnated constitutes the challenge of being human. In the midst of the immensity of life and death, in which billions of us perhaps fulfill some cosmological function by our birth, suffering, and dying, each one of us is invited to fulfill the purpose of our unique incarnation. Using a metaphor from the gospels, the question raised by spiritual traditions is: Lambs of nature as we are in any case, how can we also become lambs of God?

In connection with the point and significance of human incarnation, there is a universal suggestion that the energy of consciousness—the soul, *jiva*, or spirit—has some purpose and intention in taking on a body. Consciousness is aware of what needs to be undertaken, and it needs a body in order to act accordingly. To use a classical analogy from *Sankhyakarika* of Ishvarakrishna: the spirit (purusha) has the vision, but is lame; the body-mind (prakriti) is blind but it can carry and move. Together they can constitute an integrated and whole person, with both the vision to see what needs to be done and the ability to carry out the corresponding action. Prakriti, although following strict causality, is alive and purposeful, and every existence, even a stone, has consciousness, which is to say it has being and purposive awareness, however rudimentary. The religious perspective understands that creation is from Above downward. In contradistinction to modern scientific cosmology, spirit precedes mind, which in its turn is prior to body. In a rightly ordered and integrated person, the formation of whom is the sole purpose of yoga, the body-mind obeys the intention and purposes of the spirit.

However, the fall of consciousness into physical birth and existence is said to be hazardous. The density of the medium of incarnation and the momentum of its own forces and tendencies are so great that whatever be the initial level of the incarnating consciousness, it begins to identify itself with the level of the body-mind at the moment of birth, and continues to do so throughout life unless reminded of its original intention and purpose by spiritual disciplines such as yoga. It is as if a hypnotic sleep overtakes the original consciousness as it descends into the body, a form of amnesia from which it needs to be woken up by those who have not forgotten. This may in fact be said to be the practical meaning of the spiritual element in a person. This element, the soul, in those beings in whom it exists, has one single property: deep down, a part of the person has a dim recollection of having come from somewhere, for some purpose, and of having forgotten one's original nature. The more developed the soul of the person is, the more clearly this true self is remembered.

There are many stories that speak about an enveloping of the human consciousness by a magical veil of illusion and fantasy, so that one is unable to remember one's true nature. Ramakrishna, a late-nineteenth-century sage from India, told a story about a tigress who attacked a flock of goats. Shot by a hunter just as she sprang on her prey, the tigress gave birth to a cub and died. The cub grew up in the company of goats. Following their example, he started eating grass and bleating like them, even when he grew to be a big tiger. One day another tiger attacked the flock and was amazed to see a grass-eating tiger in the flock. When the wild tiger caught up to the grass-eating tiger, the latter began to bleat. The wild tiger dragged the other to the water and asked him to look at his face in the water and see that it was identical to his own. He gave a little meat to the bleating tiger, who had difficulty eating it. Gradually, however, the grass-eating tiger got to know the taste of blood, and came to relish the meat, then the wild tiger said: "Now you see there is no difference between you and me; come along and follow me into the forest."

We can well imagine the jungle-reverberating sound of two free tigers roaring! We have forgotten our true nature, our wild roar, and we bleat as if we were goats. When we remember ourselves, it is like the prodigal son when he came to himself: this, our brother, was dead and is alive again, was lost and is found.

It is said in Valmiki's *Ramayana* that even the god Rama, whose sole purpose in taking an earthly incarnation was to deliver human beings from the great demon Ravana and to lead them in the path of dharma, forgot his true nature and purpose, until he was reminded by Shiva, the master of sleep and lord of yoga.

It is worth remarking that every religious tradition, including those traditions such as Christianity which do not in general accept reincarnation, believes in the principle of body-soul causality: what a person does in and with this body affects the quality of the soul and its destiny in the life to come. Thus the possibility of evolution of the soul exists in all traditions. In those religions which accept reincarnation, this evolution of the soul corresponds to its manifestation in subtler and subtler bodies or forms. If the needs of the energy of consciousness in response to which it incarnated were met by the person during this life, the energy can move to higher levels of intention and purpose in the cosmic scheme—at the summit of which is Brahman, Om, or Shunyata—and take on further incarnations in correspondingly subtler levels of materiality than our own body-minds. If a person does not accomplish the purpose of the present incarnation, the energy of consciousness which was incarnated returns to its own level at the death of the body-mind. But the particular human incarnation has been wasted.

The energy of consciousness carries its needs and purposes, which cannot be accomplished without some material form. Therefore, there will be another incarnation at the same level of materiality, and the process will repeat itself endlessly. Thus one is condemned to reincarnation, not only to *re-birth* but also to *re-death* at the same level of body-mind until one is freed of that level by giving heed to and discharging the demands of the spirit. This process will go on until the energy of consciousness evolves to the highest level, that of pure consciousness without materiality, and therefore the question of incarnation or reincarnation out of any compulsive or causal necessity does not arise. However, from that level of freedom a Bodhisattva or the Logos or Krishna may be incarnated out of love or compassion for creatures. At the intermediate levels of consciousness, if a person is stuck at any given level, such a person is condemned to be immortal at that level and must live for ever. If immortality is understood to mean a continued existence in time, usually projected by the mind out of a momentum of the known and a fear of the unknown, then reincarnation at the same level and form, say on the earth, presents a perfect prison of immortality, a vicious circle from which there is no escape. This is not a doctrine of hope or reassurance, any more than it would be comforting for a very sick person, wishing for health or for death, to be told that they would continue to live in the present state for ever. What is *eternal* is not *everlasting*, nor the other way around. Moments of eternal presence take place in time but only in the now of awareness, and they indicate a level of consciousness rather than an extension in time. An endless extension in time is not what can bring about the level of eternal life or a freedom from fear or sorrow or time.

The Bhagavad Gita (2:12–30) offers the classical statement concerning reincarnation, which is no more a mystery than incarnation is in the first place. At the deepest essential core of every human being, nay of everything, is the same energy as at the highest level on the spectrum of consciousness. This essential Self—that is, Atman, which according to the resounding enunciation of the Upanishads is identically one with Brahman—takes on bodies which take birth and die, but Itself is not born and does not die at any time; It is eternal, indestructible, and everlasting. What is born, ages, and dies is the body-mind, not the true Self. Just as a person gives up worn-out clothes and puts on other new ones, similarly the embodied gives up decrepit bodies and takes on new ones.

The question to be raised in the perspective which I have been trying to outline here is not whether consciousness can survive bodily death. The body could not live, and nothing could exist, without consciousness. Furthermore, the question is not even whether consciousness can survive bodily birth and existence. What lives in the body is consciousness. The question is whether a person, while being pulled by the large momentum and force of the automaton of the body-mind, can remember why consciousness took on this body and whether the body is fulfilling its purpose.

When we remember, at that moment our consciousness is at a

level higher than that of our automaton. In remembering ourselves, we know the original face before we were born. When Shiva performs his eternal dance of transformation and liberation, he dances on the head of Muyalaka, the demon of forgetfulness.

Is the Everlasting Eternal?

He that loveth his life shall lose it; and he that hateth his life in this world shall keep it unto life eternal (John 12:25).

The *everlasting* is generally understood to refer to an unlimited extension of the time coordinate, allowing a temporal entity to last for ever. When a person hopes for everlasting life, usually a sort of quantitative extension in time is hoped for. However, this is a projection based on a fear of the loss of personal ego. The continuation of the ego in the known form is wished for because the ego is not related to a larger and more cosmic dimension of the self and of reality. This profounder relationship, which is possible only in heightened states of consciousness, is what defines the *eternal*. The eternal is not opposed to time, nor is it a continuity in time; it is rather orthogonal to time. The eternal is an aspect of the quality of being rather than of temporality.

Extending Time

The eternal cannot be approached except by sacrificing the wish for the everlasting. When I wish to have a life without end, it is in fact a wish for a continuity of my personal identity, my own ego-self, throughout time. This wish arises out of a fear of the loss of my ego. It is difficult for me to imagine life, or the cosmos, without my ego being present. Because I am self-occupied, I regard myself as the center of the universe and, in my ego-centered imagination, I believe that the whole universe would collapse if I were to cease existing in the form I know. I project my fear of the loss of the known onto the unknown and I devise whole systems of consolation which would vouchsafe an everlasting life for me.

The wish for continuity, the tendency to repeat myself and the inertia of a psychological momentum prevent my transformation, being born of the Spirit. This feature of the mind is what is called *abhinivesha* by Patañjali in the *Yoga Sutra* (2:9). The usual interpretation of abhinivesha is that is a wish for a continuation of life, which in turn is often interpreted as a fear of death. However, abhinivesha is any desire for the continuation of the status quo which results in a fear of change. The wish for everlasting life is a consequence of abhinivesha and it stands in the way of the spiritual transformation necessary to find eternal life. The spiritual masters have said (see, for example, Matthew 10:39, Luke 11:33, John 12:25) that only the person who is willing to sacrifice the superficial life (or self, or ego, or *samsara*) can find Life (or Self, or God, or *Nirvana*).

Spiritual traditions do speak about the continuation of personal identity in time, but their concern is primarily with the quality of life—here and now, and not only after physical death.

In the Bhagavad Gita, Krishna declares:

> *I proclaimed this imperishable teaching (yoga) to Vivasvan*
> *He taught it to Manu, and he, to Ikshvaku.*
> *Handed down in this way from one to another,*
> *This yoga was known by the sage-kings,*
> *But, Arjuna, it became lost on earth with the lapse of time.*
> *This very yoga of old is being taught by me to you today.*
> *For you are devoted to me and my friend,*
> *And this yoga is, indeed, the supreme secret. (BG 4:1–3)*

Arjuna has not yet realized the true nature of Krishna, and he is quite understandably puzzled about Krishna's relationship with time. He asks:

> *Later was your birth, earlier was the birth of Vivasvan:*
> *How am I to understand this,*
> *That you proclaimed this teaching in the beginning? (BG 4:4)*

Krishna replies:

> *Many are my past lives and yours, Arjuna;*

I know them all, you do not, Foe-Destroyer.
Though I am unborn and of changeless self,
Though I am Lord of beings,
having taken my stand over my own prakriti
I am born by my own self's power (maya). (BG 4:5–6)

Earlier Krishna had said,

Never was there a time when I was not,
Nor you nor these rulers of men;
And never hereafter shall there be
A time when any of us will not be. (BG.2:12)

Here is a clear statement about the continuity of personal identity through time across the boundaries of life and death. Even though Arjuna and, like him, most human beings are not aware of their previous births nor of their future existences, the sages know of them, "for to one born, death is certain, and to one dying, birth is certain" (BG 2:27). Each human being is assured of immortality. In fact, we are condemned to a continuity in time for ever, in which we are imprisoned everlastingly in our own selfhood.

If we move from the Eastern perspective to a Christian one, in spite of many differences we find a similar situation in this important aspect, namely, that a person is condemned to immortality. A person does not disappear after death into total annihilation, but continues. And therein lies the dread, as well as the hope, for one may be cast into everlasting hell, though one hopes for everlasting heaven.

Nor dread nor hope attend
A dying animal;
A man awaits his end
Dreading and hoping all.
—W. B. Yeats, "Death"

It is important to emphasize that, contrary to the general popular impression, religious traditions do not refer to the mere continuity of personal identity in time across the boundary of physical death, as a promise. Such a quantitative extension in time, without a change in the quality of life, is rather a threat. Death does not lead to final extinction, as some might even wish and hope, and therefore cannot resolve the issues of life. Each of us is obliged to face the consequences of our personal actions precisely because of the continuity of the person after death. There is no escape from ourselves, for as we sow so shall we reap. The realization of a continuity of identity in time is rather a sobering fact. A philosophic life or a good life can be a preparation for life after death because of this continuity.

The Indian tradition says that life after death, in another incarnation, will be more or less a repetition of this life, with superficial changes. The body is changed, just as the clothing which is worn out might be (BG 2:22). Unless there is a radical transformation in the being of the person, unless the wearer changes deeply and essentially, only the clothes will be different. Those who see below the surface—as does Yama, the god of death and of law, and as we do when we see ourselves in the mirror of our own conscience—are not fooled by appearances. The changes in the physical body as it ages, or the change of bodies through different incarnations, do not mean that there have been changes in the essential nature and the persistent tendencies that identify the person.

Similarly, in the Christian tradition, the quality of life after death depends upon the quality of life before death, for no one can come to God who is not radically transformed by the Spirit. Christ said, "In truth, in very truth, I tell you, no one can see the kingdom of God unless he is begotten from Above ... no one can enter the kingdom of God without being begotten of water and Spirit. Flesh begets flesh, Spirit begets spirit" (John 3:3–6). If a person loses the opportunity for transformation in the incarnated state—as is also understood in the Indian traditions where incarnation is said to be necessary for spiritual evolution—then there is a continuation of the untransformed state of being. Those who are trapped in their own selfhood, in self-occupation, which is the exact opposite of the state of true love, remain exiled from the presence of God. Those who are aware of the fact of their exile, because they have sometimes experienced a different state of being, suffer the torments of hell. Only those who have sometimes sensed the possibility of vastness can truly suffer in the prison of their smallness, just as only those who have sometimes seen know the agony of blindness.

Transcending Time

If an everlasting continuity of personal identity is not what the spiritual seeker wishes, what is the aim? There is an ancient Vedic prayer, quoted in the Brihadaranyaka Upanishad, which says:

> *From the unreal lead me to the Real*
> *From darkness lead me to Light*
> *From death lead me to Life. (I.3:28)*

This state of nondeath, of Life (*amrita*), presumably is not the state in which one is born again and again, endlessly, for this continued existence is guaranteed to all and requires no effort. Such a state cannot be the goal of spiritual life, any more than death can be the aim, for the simple reason that everyone will undergo this fate in any case. On the contrary, the desired end is a state of being that does not come about automatically, but requires strenuous effort and discipline, a yoga from below as well as grace from Above.

A spiritual seeker wishes for a transformation of being that would radically alter the quality of the relationship with higher energies and levels. This transformation results in a life that is not ego-centered but is centered in God, who because of his omnipresence lives in the deepest recesses of the seeker, as well as in every other person and in every other thing. A mark of this inner reorientation in the aspirant is a shift from being in a state of occupation with acquisition and self-advancement to one of love for others and of wishing to be of service.

The highest form of sacrifice is the renunciation of the ego-self. Our one individual and personal possession is the sense of 'I'; all other possessions are accidental and subject to external loss. This self which is occupied with itself is what the spiritual aspirant undertakes to surrender. The saints achieve only this: they succeed in doing nothing. Nothing, that is, which is their own. They have no project, no point of view, no ambition of their own; they do what they must under the guidance of the will of God, as a service and as an offering. "In truth, in very truth I tell you, the Son can do nothing by himself; he does only what he sees the Father doing: what the Father does, the Son does. ... The teaching that I give is not my own; it is the teaching of him who sent me. Anyone whose teaching is only his own is bent on self-glorification" (John 5:19; 7:16,17). And St. Paul said, "I live, yet no longer I, but Christ liveth in me" (Galatians 2:20).

The greatest fear of the saints is that of dying without being self-annihilated, without having died to their ego-selves. Without this death they would be condemned to the prison of their own egos. As the *Theologia Germanica* (Chapter 34) says, "Nothing burneth in hell except self-will." The sage strives for a discontinuity of the ego-self in time and not for its everlasting perpetuation. Very different sorts of questions about life after death arise for those who wish to be free of their own self-will than for those who fear the extinction of their egos. The sage fears dying without the extinction of the ego, without self-naughting, without having entered into the state of Eternal Life, of Nirvana.

Krishna says in the Bhagavad Gita:

When the seer perceives no doer other than
the gunas (constituents of nature)
And knows what is higher than the gunas,
Such a one attains to my being.
Having gone beyond these three gunas
springing from the body,
The embodied one, released from birth and death, old
age, and unhappiness,
Attains immortality (amrita). (BG 14:19–20)

This state of 'immortality', of being freed from the cycle of birth and death, is certainly not a continuation of personal identity in time. This state is rather one of freedom from the limiting self—and therefore from fear and ambition, which are the marks and supports of the ego—as well as from the limitations of time.

The sun does not shine on it, nor the moon nor fire;
Those who come to this, my supreme dwelling-place,
They do not return. (BG 15:6)

Only those can come to God who do not bring themselves. No one who is anyone is fit to be one with God. As Christ said, "And no one has gone up to Heaven except he who came down from Heaven": (John 3:13). Krishna declares as a summation of his entire teaching in the Bhagavad Gita,

Having forsaken the sense of I, might, insolence,
Desire, anger, possession;
Unselfish and at peace,
One is fit to become Brahman.
Having become Brahman, tranquil in the self,
One neither grieves, nor desires;
Regarding all beings as equal,
One attains supreme dedication to me.
Through this dedication,
One knows me in essence;
Then having known me essentially,
One forthwith enters into me.
Ever performing all actions,
Taking refuge in me, By my grace,
One reaches the eternal, imperishable abode.
Renouncing all action to me with your mind,
Intent on me, relying on the yoga of understanding.
Become constantly mindful of me.

Mindful of me, you will cross all obstacles by my grace.
But if, due to your sense of I, you will not pay heed,
You will perish. (BG 18:53–58)

In order to experience the realm of the eternal or the timeless, a reorientation of the ego is needed—not a physical death. Awakening brings a freedom from the tyranny of time, which keeps us living in the past and in the future; awakening brings the possibility of living in the present, now, radically open. Eternity contains time within it, just as a cube includes a square. A consciousness viewing our temporal world from an eternal and universal point of view is not limited by our notions of temporal or causal sequence. To it, past and future events are as clearly comprehensible as the present ones; events far away are as clearly visible as near ones. In his sermon *Adolescens, tibi dico: surge!*, Meister Eckhart says, "Yesterday I said something that would seem truly incredible. I said: 'Jerusalem is as near to my soul as the place where I am now standing. Yes, in all truth; what is even more than a thousand miles farther than Jerusalem is as near to my soul as my own body; and I am as sure of this as I am of being a man.'"

The temporal order—past, present, and future—does not describe or limit the state of being. Whatever is eternal is always present, without beginning or end in time—unborn and undying. "Everything stands in a present now" (Eckhart). Those who live in the present, which is to say those who are alive and awake to the moment—which has to do with a quality of awareness rather than with any external time—have a possibility of contacting the eternal order. As Wittgenstein said: "If we take eternity to mean not infinite temporal duration but timelessness, then eternal life belongs to those who live in the present" (*Tractatus Logico Philosophicus*, proposition 6.4311).

A person for whom the ego-identity, which claims "I am this" or "I am that," is no longer the central motivating force of life, but who is cleansed in the supreme identity of oneness with Brahman or God or Suchness, can say simply "I AM." "I AM" is a sacred name of God and the experience of this state is at the threshold of God. It is the same as an experience of "God IS" and of the eternal. Even though our ordinary rationality experiences this as a transgression, the sage can truly say as Christ did: "In truth, in very truth, I tell you, before Abraham was, I AM" (John 8:58). No wonder the text adds, "Then they picked up stones to throw at Jesus."

As long as we confine ourselves to our egoistic selves, we restrict our consciousness to a small aperture in the vast spectrum of consciousness. If we widen the doors of our perception, we will be able to see more clearly than we ordinarily do. One who is awakened to the Spirit dwells both in time and in eternity. Although in time, such a person is not restricted by it. Eternity is a quality of being, rather than an extension of temporality, and it is neither an infinite extension of time nor is it in opposition to it. Eternity is quite orthogonal to time in the mathematical sense: it intersects with the dimension of time, but is not at all contained in it. No description exclusively in terms of time can adequately comprehend eternity, just as no combination of lines in two dimensions can produce a cube. In that sense, the eternal is timeless. Another dimension of consciousness is needed to live in eternity. As long as we remain confined to our ordinary consciousness, we experience and move only in time, having only vague and occasional hints of eternity.

Men's curiosity searches past and future
And clings to that dimension. But to apprehend
The point of intersection of the timeless
With time, is an occupation for the saint—
No occupation either, but something given
And taken, in a lifetime's death in love,
Ardour and selflessness and self-surrender.

—*T. S. Eliot,*
"The Dry Salvages" in Four Quartets

Yoga in the *Yoga Sutra* and the Bhagavad Gita

The Royal Yoga

According to Patañjali's *Yoga Sutra*, the classical text on yoga, the purpose of yoga is to lead to a silence of the mind (1.2). This silence is a necessary condition for the mind to be able to accurately reflect objective reality without introducing its own subjective distortions. Yoga does not create this reality, which is above the mind, but only prepares the mind to apprehend it by assisting in the transformation of the mind from an ordinary mind—full of noise, like a whole army of frenzied and drunken monkeys—to a still mind.

This transformation is not brought about by any effort or practice, as the *Yoga Sutra* (4.2–3) reminds us, for it is an unfolding of nature's own potential tendency. The practice and discipline are necessary only for removing the obstacles to this unfolding, just as a gardener removes the weeds for the sake of a healthy crop. The attempt to eliminate the obstacles to the natural unfolding and development of the human being is made through yoga, and this attempt is made so that the person's true and real nature may be realized. This real nature is independent of the contingent conditioning of space-time, thought-feeling, fear-pleasure, and form-species. In other words, the real being, called purusha, is independent of all the forces and controls of prakriti, the realm of causality and nature, both subtle and gross. The real is above and behind the actual. The sole purpose not only of human incarnation but of the whole of prakriti, as the *Yoga Sutra* (2.21) tells us, is for the realization of purusha. Enlightenment and freedom are in this realization alone.

Yoga is one of the six classical darshanas (perspectives, visions) for the attainment of ultimate reality. Out of these six schools of Indian philosophy, the school of *Samkhya* is often associated with yoga, and the two are frequently coupled together. There does not seem to be much basis for this association, for Yoga and Samkhya have represented two distinct approaches for a very long time, even though there are some similarities in their underlying cosmologies. On the other hand, all the schools of thought in India, even the ones opposed to Yoga in its metaphysical doctrines, such as the school of Vedanta, have recognized the great value of the practical aspects of yoga. Dating from a period prior to the ascendancy of the Aryans in India, yoga has had an enormous influence on all forms of Indian spirituality, including the Buddhist and Jain, and later on the Sufi and the Christian. Yoga can be said to constitute the very essence of practical spirituality of India.

The word 'yoga' is derived from the root *yuj*, which means to unite or to join together, much like the etymological meaning of the word 'religion'. The practice of yoga may lead to the union of the human and the divine within the self. It is a way to wholeness and to an integration of all aspects and levels of oneself. Yoga is not just a collection of certain practices devoid of a metaphysical basis, but it is based upon a perfectly structured and integrated worldview which aims at the transformation of a human being from the actual and unrefined form to a perfected form. The prakrita (literally 'natural', 'common', 'vulgar', 'unrefined') state is one in which a person compulsively repeats actions, in reaction to the forces of prakriti, which are active both outside and inside the person. Through yoga a person can become sanskrita (literally, 'well made', 'well put together', 'refined') and thus no longer be wholly at the mercy of natural forces and inclinations. It can be said that yoga leads to a freedom from nature, including the freedom from human nature; its aim is transcendence of human nature into pure being.

Yoga is concerned with being (sat) and knowing (jñana) as well as doing (karma), and therefore it cannot be classified exclusively as religion or science or art. The aim of yoga, however, is beyond these three and beyond any opposites they imply. Mythologically, Yoga is sometimes personified as the son of Dharma and Kriya. Dharma is essentially the order that is the support of the cosmos, and Kriya, as action and performance, is a shakti (energy, power) of Vishnu in one of his incarnations. The importance of yoga in the Indian tradition is obvious: a name or an epithet of

Shiva is Yoganatha; of Vishnu, Yogapati; and of Krishna, Yogeshvara; in each case meaning essentially "the master or lord of Yoga." Without the mastery of yoga, indeed, nothing can be accomplished rightly. As the Yogashikha Upanishad (1.67) says: "Verily there is no merit higher than Yoga, no good higher than Yoga, no subtlety higher than Yoga; there is nothing that is higher than Yoga."

The Central Yoga

Although there are many kinds of yoga, such as karma yoga (the yoga of works) and bhakti yoga (the yoga of love), the Indian tradition has in general maintained that there is only one yoga, with varying emphases on different aspects and methods employed in various schools of yoga. The most authoritative text of classical yoga is the *Yoga Sutra*, *Aphorisms of Yoga* (abbreviated as YS), the compilation of which is attributed to Patañjali. Nothing very much is known about Patañjali, not even when he lived. It is possible that the *Yoga Sutra* text was compiled sometime between the second century BCE and the fourth century CE. In any case, there is no question that most of the ideas and practices mentioned in the *Yoga Sutra* were already familiar to the gurus (teachers) of Indian spirituality, who passed them on to their disciples with appropriate instructions and initiations. As is the mark of the *sutra* (literally, thread) literature, the *Yoga Sutra* presents the ideas in an extremely terse manner, leaving it to the individual teacher to expound the ideas more fully for a circle of disciples. In the process, no doubt each teacher emphasizes the aspects regarded as most useful.

The aim of yoga is set out in the beginning of the *Yoga Sutra*, in its most celebrated and most debated aphorism (1.2), namely, *Yogah chittavritti nirodhah* (Yoga is the removal of the fluctuations of consciousness). One practices yoga to steady the attention, which is constantly undergoing fluctuations (*vritti*). These fluctuations may be pleasant or unpleasant, but they are, in either case, distractions from the steady attention of a quiet mind. These vrittis are grouped under five headings by Patañjali, corresponding to the activities of the ordinary mind, namely, *pramana* (judging, comparing, discursive activity), *viparyaya* (misjudging, misperception), *vikalpa* (verbal association, imagination), *nidra* (dreaming, sleeping), and smriti (memory arising from past experience). According to an underlying assumption of yoga, the mind, which is confined to the above modes, is limited in scope and cannot know the objective truth about anything. The mind is not the true knower: it can infer or quote authority or make hypotheses or speculate about the nature of reality, but it cannot see objects directly—from the inside, as it were, as they really are in themselves. In order to allow direct seeing to take place, the mind, which by its very nature attempts to mediate between the object and the subject, has to be quieted. When the mind is totally silent and totally alert, both the subject (purusha) and the object (prakriti) are simultaneously present to it: the seer is there; what is to be seen is there; and the seeing takes place without distortion. Then there is no comparing or judging, no misunderstanding, no fantasizing, no dozing off in heedlessness, nor any clinging to past knowledge. There is simply the seeing. That state is called *kaivalya* (literally, aloneness). It is not the aloneness of the seer separated from the seen, as is unfortunately far too often maintained as a goal of yoga, but the aloneness of seeing in its purity, without any distortions introduced by the organs of perception, namely, the mind, the heart, and the senses. The aim of yoga is clear seeing, which is the sole power of the seer (YS 2.20) and only of the seer (purusha), not of the mind.

It is of utmost importance, from the point of view of yoga, to distinguish between the mind (chitta) and the real seer (purusha). Chitta pretends to know, but it is in the realm of the known and the seen. The misidentification between the seer (subject) and the seen (object)—which is mistaking chitta with its fluctuations and its sorrows for purusha, which is without sorrow and without alterations—is the fundamental error from which all other problems and suffering arise (YS 3.17). This basic ignorance is what gives rise to *asmita* (I-am-this-ness or egoism). This is a limitation by particularization: purusha says "I am"; asmita says "I am this" or "I am that." The strong desire to perpetuate the personal self and the resulting separation from all else, which manifests as a wish for continuation (abhinivesha) of this separate entity, comes from this egoism. This wish is maintained by indulging in "I-like-this" (*raga*, attraction) or

"I-do-not-like-this" (*dvesha*, aversion). Freedom from the fundamental ignorance leading to all sorrow is achieved by an unceasing vision of discernment (*viveka-khyati*). This vision of discernment alone can permit transcendental insight (*prajña*) to arise. Nothing can force the appearance of this insight; all one can do is to prepare the ground for it. Since it is said that the whole purpose for the existence of the mind as well as the rest of prakriti is to serve purusha, if the ground is properly prepared, prajña is likely to arise.

The ground to be prepared is the entire psychosomatic organism, sharira, for it is through the whole organism that purusha sees and prajña arises, not the mind alone nor the heart nor the physical body by itself. One with dulled senses has as little chance of coming to prajña as one with a stupid mind or with an unfeeling heart. Agitation in any part of the entire organism causes a fluctuation of attention. And every act, including mental acts like thought, volition, and intention, leaves an impression (*samskara*) on the psyche, which in turn lodges itself in the various tensions, postures, and gestures of the physical body. These impressions in turn create tendencies (*vasana*) which dispose one toward certain sorts of actions. The really deep tendencies cut across the boundaries of what we ordinarily call life and death—that is, the life and death of the physical body. This, in short, is the law of karma (action, work): as one acts, so one becomes; and as one is, so one acts. It is less to say that one reaps what one sows; it is more to say, in accordance with the ideas of yoga, that every act makes a person a little different from before, and this different person now naturally acts according to the tendencies of the new being. Within the realm of prakriti and karma, a person is not anything except their actions, thoughts, feelings, and all the conditioning of the past. A person is an expression of the working out of the law of karma. One repeats oneself helplessly, at the same level, neurotically, precisely because one does not know what one does and why. But just as there is a cosmic tendency for this mechanical repetition (*pravritti*), there is also a cosmic tendency for waking up to our real situation (*nivritti*) which can free us from a repetition of the past.

The effort required, with the ultimate aim of coming to the vision of discernment (viveka-khayati), which alone may lead to true insight (prajña), is enormously difficult, for the simple reason that a total cleansing of the deepest recesses of our entire consciousness is required. Otherwise, subtle impressions and tendencies will reassert themselves, leading us into a repetitious circle. What is needed is a flow (*pratipрrasava*) counter to the ordinary tendencies of prakriti, a turning around (*metanoia* in Greek, usually translated as 'repentance' in the New Testament). It is only by a reversal of the usual tendencies of the mind that its agitations can be quietened. Then the mind can know its right and proper place with respect to the purusha, as the *known* rather than the *knower* (YS 2.10; 4.18–22). However pure and refined the mind is, in the terminology of the *Yoga Sutra*, even if the mind is constituted of pure satva (luminosity, purity), it is distinct from purusha and is radically inferior to it in its power of seeing.

The Limbs of Yoga

The usual tendencies of the mind are countered through the eight limbs of Yoga by steady practice (*abhyasa*) and increasing inwardness (*vairagya*). Elsewhere, in YS 2.1–2, a different scheme is indicated: austerity, self-study, and devotion to *Ishvara* (the Lord) constitute Kriya yoga, which has as its purpose the lessening of the causes-of-sorrow (*kleshas*) and the cultivation of *samadhi* (settled intelligence, silence). Here we shall follow the much more elaborated scheme (YS 2.28–55; 3.1–8) of the eight limbs: *yama*, *niyama*, *asana*, *pranayama*, *pratyahara*, *dharana*, *dhyana*, and *samadhi*. The first one, yama, refers to the various self-restraints, which include abstention from violence, falsehood, theft, incontinence, and acquisitiveness. The second limb, niyama, consists in the observances of purity, contentment, austerity, self-study, and devotion to Ishvara. (These last three observances are the same that were said earlier to constitute kriya yoga). The third and fourth limbs, asana and pranayama, are concerned with the right posture, which makes one both relaxed and alert, and with the proper regulation of breathing for steadying the attention. These two limbs by themselves are often elaborated in terms of numerous postures and breathing exercises in schools of hatha yoga, the yoga of force. In the physical culture aspect of yoga, sometimes one encounters great displays of ascetic prowess, which have nothing to do with the purpose of yoga. The fifth limb, pratyahara, is the inward turning of the senses so that they can be freed of the external impressions in order to obey the mind.

These five limbs constitute the outer group from the total eight limbs of yoga, the other three being the more inner limbs. Dharana is concentration in which the consciousness is bound to a single spot; dhyana is contemplation or meditative absorption in which there is an uninterrupted flow of attention from the observer to the observed. So far the observer has acted as the center of consciousness which sees. When the observing is done by purusha, through the mind emptied of itself, that state is called samadhi, a state of silence and of settled intelligence. In this state the mind does not introduce its own distortions, and the object can be known truly, as it is. This is an inversion of the usual mode of knowing, in which the mind receives the impressions about the object from the senses and imposes its own fluctuations (vṛittis) upon the object. In samadhi, the mind acts as the arena in which there is no subjective or personal center of consciousness that can introduce any distortion of the object; there is only the pure seeing. No agency or organ mediates between the object and the seeing. Thus, the insight obtained in the state of samadhi is neither sensual nor mental, nor has it to do with feelings. It is not personal knowledge, nor is it subjective. It refers wholly and exclusively to the object; it is completely objective insight—of the object as it is and as it chooses to reveal itself, without any violation or forcing from the observer—for, at the moment of pure seeing, the observer as a separated center of consciousness does not exist. As the *Yoga Sutra* says (1.48–49; 2.15; 3.54), the insight in the state of samadhi is truth-bearing (*ritambhara*). The scope of this insight is different from the scope of the knowledge gained from tradition or inference. Unlike the latter knowledge, the insight of prajña reveals the unique particularity, rather than an abstract generality, of the object. For this reason, mystical insight is often considered closer to sense perception rather than discursive knowledge; it is clear, however, that in prajña the senses are extremely refined and turned inward and do not mediate between the seer and the object. Unlike mental knowledge, in which there is an opposition between the object and the modalities of the mind, an opposition that inevitably leads to sorrow, the insight of prajña, born of a sustained vision of discernment, is said to be the deliverer. Prajña can pertain to any object, large or small, far or near, and to any time, past, present or future, for it is without time sequence, present everywhere at once.

It may be remarked that the various steps of yoga are ordered yet are not sequentially linear. The completion of one step is not required before the next one can be undertaken. Some of the apparent linearity arises from the analytical and linguistic nature of the exposition. Earlier steps are preparatory to the later ones, but they are not absolutely necessary. Nor are they completely sufficient, for they do not determine the later steps. A right physical posture or moral conduct may aid internal development but it does not guarantee it. More often, the external behavior reflects the internal development. As an example, a person does not necessarily become wise by breathing or thinking in a particular way; a person breathes and thinks in that way because of their level of wisdom

The three inner limbs of yoga, namely, dharana, dhyana, and samadhi, together constitute what is called *samyama* (discipline, constraint). It is the application of samyama to any object which leads to the direct perception (*sakshatkara*) of it because in the state of quietude in which the vrittis are removed, the chitta is like a transparent jewel taking on the true color of the object which fuses (*samapatti*) with it (YS 1.41). The special attention which prevails in the state of samyama can be brought to bear on any aspect of prakriti, which, as was said earlier, encompasses all that can be an object of perception, however subtle.

The basic research method of the natural science of yoga is to bring a completely quiet mind and to wait without agitation or projection, letting the object reveal itself in its own true nature. This science is further extended by the principles of analogy and isomorphism between the macrocosmos and the microcosmos which is the human organism. A particularly striking example of this isomorphism is to be found in the Yoga Darshana Upanishad, where the external mountains and other places are identified with the various parts of the organism. The external *tirtha* (sacred ford, holy water, place of pilgrimage) is considered inferior to the tirtha in the body.

The Mount Meru is in the head
and Kedara in your brow;
between your eyebrows, near your nose,
know, dear disciple, that Varanasi stands;
in your heart is the confluence
of the Ganges and the Yamuna;
lastly, Kamalalya
is to be found in the muladhara,

To prefer external tirthas
to those concealed in your body,
is to prefer common potsherds
to diamonds laid in your hands.

Your sins will be washed away,
whether you have made love with your wife
or even with your own daughter,
if you carry out the pilgrimages
within your own body from one tirtha to another.

True yogis who worship the atman in themselves
have no need of water tirthas
or of gods of wood and clay.

The tirthas of your body
infinitely surpass those of the world,
and the tirtha-of-the-soul is the greatest of them:
the others are nothing beside it.

—*Yoga Darshana Upanishad (4.48–53)*

Yoga and Power

A large number of aphorisms in the *Yoga Sutra* (3.16–53) describe the knowledge and the powers gained by attending to various objects in the state of samyama. For example, we are told that through samyama on the sun, one gains insight into the solar system, and by samyama on the moon, knowledge of the arrangement of the stars (YS 3.26–27). Similarly, many occult or extraordinary powers, *siddhis*, accrue to the yogi by bringing the state of samyama to bear on various aspects of oneself: for example, by samyama on the relation between the ear and ether, one acquires the divine ear by which one can hear at a distance or hear extremely subtle and usually inaudible sounds. Many other powers are mentioned by Patañjali; however, none of them is his main concern. These powers may be present from birth or they may be acquired by other means such as drugs or mantras (literally, 'mind-instrument'; special sounds usually given by a teacher to the disciple for recitation) or physical austerities (YS 4.1). There is no suggestion that there is anything wrong with these powers, nor is there a suggestion that there is anything wrong with the mind as it is. The point is more that the mind, as it is, is an inadequate instrument for true knowledge; similarly, these powers, however vast, are inadequate as the goal of true knowledge. The yogis who get preoccupied with them are likely to get sidetracked from the true path of yoga. Therefore, these powers are seen as temptations and, along with heightened sensory experiences, are regarded as obstacles to sustained samadhi (YS 3.36–37).

The Spirituality of Yoga Discipline

The real seer is purusha, which is not personally mine or yours; it is the pure power of seeing. In yoga, as a continuation of the Vedic sacrifice (yajña), the sacrifice of the limiting mind is required for the sake of an unlimited power to see. Sacrifice of the separated self, with all of its fears and hopes, likes and dislikes, sorrows and pleasures, failures and ambitions is needed for the sake of the Only One who truly sees. Then the sacrifice of the seen for the sake of the Only One who truly is follows. This comes about in *nirbija samadhi* (seedless silence), when there is no object separated from the purusha, there is no subject separated from the purusha, there is no knowing except the purusha. The seer, the seen, and the seeing are all One; there is no other. This is the state of kaivalya, of aloneness, not because there is an opposition or a separation but simply because there is no other. With respect to this state of samadhi, the previously labeled inner limbs of yoga are also outer. This samadhi is also called *dharma-megha-samadhi* (silence in the cloud of right order). Thence follows the ending of all the causes of sorrow, of all the blemishes and imperfections; little remains to be known, for the insight in this state is infinite; the purpose of the human incarnation is fulfilled and the yogi is completely free and established in the pure awareness of purusha (YS 4.29–34).

In this movement from the personal self to the Self, from the identification with chitta to the identification with purusha, right internal order is established. The sacrifice (from the Latin *sacre facere*, 'to make sacred') of chitta and prakriti for the sake of purusha is precisely what renders them sacred and gives them significance. In this process of transformation, many stages and their corresponding levels of silence are described in the *Yoga Sutra*. As a whole, the process of yoga allows the emergence of purusha from within the psychosomatic organism, as a sculpture is released from the stone by chiseling and discarding. The organism, or prakriti in general, is no more an impediment to purusha than the stone is to the sculpture. Nor is prakriti considered unreal or a mental projection. Everything in prakriti is considered as alive: she is very real, and though she can overwhelm the mind with her dynamism and charms and veil the truth, yet in her proper place and function she exists in order to serve purusha.

The discipline of yoga is against the ordinary current. All the eight limbs of yoga place constraints on the usual activity of our desires, inclinations, body, breath, senses, mind, attention, and ego, so that they may be brought under the control of something higher. The more controlled and quieted these various aspects of ourselves are, the greater is the development of the vision of discernment. This, in its turn, leads to the removal of ignorance about our true identity. Then we realize that we have been identifying ourselves only with our mental-physical self, which is of the nature of the object rather than the real seer. When this misidentification is broken and we no longer rely on the mind for true insight, the natural conflict between the whole and the part—that is, between what is and the projections of the mind—is dissolved. This leads to the removal of sorrow and its underlying causes, and to the cultivation of a deeper and deeper silence, and finally to the aloneness of pure awareness.

Many Yogas

What we have described so far is the classical and central yoga, sometimes called the *raja Yoga* (the Royal Yoga). Kriya-yoga, noted in the *Yoga Sutra* (YS 2.1–2), which consists of austerity, self-study, and devotion to the Lord; and hatha yoga, which focuses on the physical culture aspect of yoga and concentrates on the asanas and pranayama, have also been briefly discussed. Many other different forms of yoga have been developed with different emphases or exaggerations of one aspect or another. For example, Patañjali mentions (YS 1.29–40) that inwardness can be cultivated and the distractions of the mind attenuated by the practice of concentration on a single principle, or by the projection of friendliness, compassion, and equanimity toward others, or by the appropriate retention and expulsion of breath, or by dwelling on those who have conquered attachment, or by attending to inner sensations. Corresponding to each one of these possible techniques, whole schools have arisen which cultivate one or the other method, which can be called a specific yoga. Over time, yoga has thus come to stand for any spiritual path, method, or technique—although, in general, the goal of all these yogas is the same as that of the central yoga, even when expressed in terms of the particular metaphysics and metaphors of their own schools.

Owing to the multifarious uses to which the word 'yoga' can be and has been put, no exhaustive list of all the yogas can be given. Among the well-known varieties are *mantra yoga*, which makes use of the recitation of special sounds usually given by a teacher to a disciple; *laya yoga*, in which one makes use of the inner sound for merging the mind into the infinite; *kundalini yoga*, which describes the whole process of yoga in terms of wakening the cosmic energy usually lying dormant coiled up at the base of the spine, so that it can rise through the various centers (*chakra*) in the subtle body, and the various yogas mentioned and elaborated in the Bhagavad Gita. The theory and the practice of kundalini yoga have been much developed in the Tantric literature, describing in detail the movements and transformation of the energies (shakti) in the body.

Yoga and the Bhagavad Gita

The Bhagavad Gita expands the use of the word 'yoga' enormously. In addition to the well-known yogas called karma yoga (yoga of action), bhakti yoga (yoga of love and devotion), and jñana yoga (yoga of knowledge), every chapter in the Bhagavad Gita ends with a colophon labeling it a yoga. For example, the first chapter ends with the colophon (not perhaps found in the earlier texts) calling it "The Yoga of Arjuna's Confusion," and the eleventh chapter is called "The Yoga of the Vision of Cosmic Form," and so on. Anything that can be made use of and harmonized with the general principles of yoga in the quest for a connection with the Absolute can be called a specific sort of yoga.

Three further remarks can be made here about the Bhagavad Gita. First, the Bhagavad Gita is absolutely essential for an understanding of yoga; it is a text par excellence on yoga, as is the *Yoga Sutra*. Second, the Bhagavad Gita extends the range and understanding of yoga in at least two different ways. By forging a link between classical yoga and other metaphysical systems and metaphors, it enlarges our vision of the scope of yoga. We are reminded by the whole setting of the battlefield, by the insistence on action in this world of prakriti, and by the presence of Krishna himself as a model yogi, that not only is there no conflict between prakriti and purusha but that, rightly seen, prakriti can and does serve the purposes of purusha. Furthermore, a free purusha, as exemplified by Krishna, acts in prakriti not from compulsion but from freedom and compassion, as and when there is a need for it.

Third, the central yoga that Krishna teaches in the Bhagavad Gita is *buddhi yoga* (the yoga of integrated intelligence and discernment), of which the various aspects are yogas such as karma yoga, bhakti yoga, and jñana yoga. The place of buddhi in the Bhagavad Gita is central. Krishna advises Arjuna to "seek refuge in buddhi" (BG 2.49). "To them who are constantly integrated worshiping me with love, I give that buddhi yoga by which they may draw near to me" (BG 10.10). Later, during the process of summing up his entire teaching, Krishna says again, "Renouncing all actions to me, making me your goal, relying on buddhi yoga, become constantly mindful of me. Mindful of me you will overcome all obstacles by my grace. But if because of self-centeredness you will not listen, you will perish" (BG 18.57–58). It is only the integrated buddhi which can have a vision of and follow dictates of purusha. Buddhi is what gives a focus to an integral yoga, for example, of the sort elaborated by Sri Aurobindo in the twentieth century, very much under the influence of the Bhagavad Gita. This is what corresponds precisely to the viveka-khyati (vision of discernment) in the *Yoga Sutra* by which alone the root ignorance can be removed.

Right Order

That which the yogis seek does not serve their own purposes. In fact, as long as we have our own purposes, we cannot really be open to higher and sacred purposes. The whole meaning of yoga can be understood as progressive freedom from the hindrances that impede our availability to the purposes of the suprapersonal intelligence. The major hindrance is what we usually call our ego or self; as long as it serves its own ends, it cannot serve the ends of the real Self.

What yoga aims at is right internal order, which is primarily vertical. Yoga takes its direction and significance from the reality that is beyond the body or the psyche. This is what renders the physio-psychology of yoga sacred. Cultivation of the body or the mind for its own sake is not yoga. The psychic healing in yoga has its center above the psyche; here the wholeness aspired to is that of holiness. Normal physical and psychological functioning is necessary but not sufficient; without the movement along the vertical spiritual axis, any adjustment in the psyche constitutes only a horizontal arrangement of subtle matter. It is the stillness of the psyche that is required so that the purusha may be heard and may hear. Patañjali had defined yoga, in terms of its procedure, as the controlling of the fluctuations of consciousness (chitta); Vyasa, in his commentary on the *Yoga Sutra* (*Yoga Bhashya* 1.1) defines yoga in terms of its aim as silence (samadhi). Then purusha abides in his own true form.

Self-Consciousness in the *Yoga Sutra*: Need for an Intermediate Self

Self-Realization and Self-Consciousness

The importance of self-knowledge or self-awareness or self-consciousness is commonly emphasized in Indian thought. It is useful to see what *self-consciousness* means in the context of Patañjali's *Yoga Sutra*, which constitutes the classical text of yoga and the heart of practical Indian spirituality, and to explore the implications of self-consciousness for spiritual practice.

The ultimate aim of yoga as expressed in the *Yoga Sutra* is Self-realization (*Atma anubhava*), not self-consciousness. The difference between self-consciousness and Self-realization is enormous—not only in theory but also for spiritual practice. Self-consciousness presupposes a separation between the self which is being observed and the observing self. It is entirely possible and practical to speak in terms of higher levels of the self observing, or being conscious of, lower levels. But yoga aims at the realization of the highest self, both in theory and in practice, and there is nothing higher than it, which could observe it. Whatever we can be conscious of is not the Self.

The Self has no characteristic other than seeing, being mindful, attending, or being aware, consciring. "The Seer is pure seeing itself, but though pure appears to see through the concepts" (YS 2.20). It is possible to call the Self (Purusha) 'Pure Consciousness', from which awareness of everything else is derived, but which itself is not an object of awareness. As the *Yoga Sutra* puts it "Yoga is the cessation of the fluctuation of attention. Then the Seer is established in its own essential nature" (1:2–3).

The Self and Self

From a practical point of view, it is not only impossible to begin from the very highest level of awareness—that of kaivalya, which is a state of total attention and of pure seeing—it is in fact harmful. It is very easy to avoid undertaking the necessary *sadhana* (practice) and *tapasya* (effort, exertion) and, instead, to make a mental substitution of the enunciation of the sages for one's own experience. Here, more than elsewhere, it is necessary to remember the caution of Vyasa in his commentary on the *Yoga Sutra* that "Yoga has to be known by yoga. Yoga manifests through yoga" (*Yoga Bhashya* III.6).

At all intermediate levels, at all levels other than the ultimate unitive state of kaivalya, it is not only possible to speak of a separated self but also necessary. There are some very pertinent verses in the Bhagavad Gita: "Raise self by self, let not the self degrade itself; for self's friend is self indeed, so too is self self's foe. Self is the friend to the person whose self is by the self controlled, but for the person bereft of self (*anatmana*), self will act as an enemy indeed. The higher self (*paramatma*) of the self-controlled is fully present in heat and cold, comfort and discomfort, in honour and disgrace" (6:5–7). It is clear that self (atman) can be spoken of at many levels—from one's bodily self to the highest Purusha.

The fact that there are many levels of the self is made clear in the story of the education of Indra, chief of the gods, and of Vairochana, chief of the antigods, by their common teacher Prajapati in the Chandogya Upanishad (VIII.7.1–12.6). Prajapati's teaching is about the nature of Atman, the real concern of any serious searcher. Indra and Vairochana had come to Prajapati to learn about the nature of the self. After a period of thirty-two years of service, Prajapati pointed to the image of Indra and Vairochana reflected in water as their self. They went away satisfied that the body, which could be adorned and glorified, was the Atman. Indra soon realized that the body does not survive after death and returned to ask Prajapati for a further teaching. After Indra served for an additional period of thirty-two years, Prajapati pointed to the level of thought and imagination as the self. Indra left satisfied that he knew the self, but soon saw that the pleasures of the mind and feeling do not last, and he returned to Prajapati again. After Indra served thirty-two more years, Prajapati pointed to a deeper level of the self which is unmoved by external circumstances. But Indra soon realized that this was not the highest level of the Self, and asked Prajapati again. After five more years, Indra realized the Self which is present in the body, but which is not the body; which sees, but is not seen; which hears but is not heard; which knows but is not known.

It is interesting that this story, in which the searchers are initially satisfied with the identification of the bodily self with the highest Atman, is usually interpreted as an indication of the dimwittedness of the aspirants. But this story much more indicates the general difficulty of spiritual evolution rather than the lack of acuity on the part of Indra. A progressive freedom from an identification of ourselves with the body-mind, and from the whole realm of prakriti, to the realization of oneness of the seer, the seen, and seeing covers the entire spectrum of spiritual awakening.

Another model indicating different levels of the self is described in terms of different levels of consciousness, divided into the *jagrata* (waking), *nidra* (sleep), sushupti (dreamless sleep), and *turiya* (the fourth). It is important to emphasize that these levels of awareness are progressively higher states of *wakefulness* and not of deeper and deeper sleep. In the jagrata state, one is awake to the world, but asleep to the Real. In the sushupti state, one can be awake to the Real, because one is deeply asleep to the world and is not troubled by it at all—unlike the nidra state, in which one regards the world as a dream but is still interested and excited by it. Turiya is beyond description and is simply referred to as 'the fourth' to indicate its difference from the other three states of consciousness. States of progressive awakening are also described in the spiritual classics such as the *Yoga Sutra* or *The Cloud of Unknowing*.

Although it is possible to jump mentally to the highest level of the Self or to the highest level of consciousness, it is necessary to experience all the levels in order for the Self to be realized. The other levels exist in order to make the realization of the highest level possible. The body-mind exists so that the Spirit may manifest and experience itself. This is a requirement of the cosmos. "The seen exists for the sake of the seer" (YS 2.21). There is no reason to believe that the existence of Prakriti is a mistake or that it is unnecessary. This is an essential point and very necessary to be stressed as a corrective to the general tendency of much of Indian thought according to which the body, or Prakriti, or the lower levels, are considered to be unnecessary or troublesome, needing to be discarded. In practice, however, it is quite clear that the body is necessary for Self-realization. That is why a human incarnation is said to be a great benediction. Even the gods have to be reborn as human beings in order to work toward the total freedom of nirvana. The Buddha invoked the Earth as a witness in his struggles with Mara. Without the earth, heaven can have no meaning. Without the body, there can be no spiritual evolution.

If we do not make the impractical error of jumping to the highest, where any sensible discourse naturally breaks down, we can consider the issue at intermediate levels of spiritual energy and awareness. For the evolution of energy at any level, an incarnation in a body is needed. However, it is the body, or the constituents (gunas) of prakriti, which evolves and is transformed (see YS 4:32), and it cannot be discarded or ignored, any more than the stone can be discarded in the making of a sculpture. It is important to understand the process of this subtle transformation in which the body (including subtler bodies) and the more aware energy of purusha come together. Nonexperiential philosophy is dangerous here if it is not accompanied by sadhana (practice), because it is very tempting to jump to the highest level and forget all the intermediate levels of subtler and subtler bodies and of finer and finer attention. It is again useful to remind ourselves of the caution of Vyasa quoted earlier, that "Yoga has to be known by yoga."

Let Me Have a Self

We need all the levels of the self, from the physical body upward. They are all ourselves, and they are all necessary for any spiritual practice. The evolution of consciousness and of the universe needs all the various levels of sharira (body) which correspond to the physical body, including manas, buddhi, and asmita. The *Yoga Sutra* says that the very existence of Prakriti is for the sake of Purusha (2:21). What does this mean? Is Purusha lacking something without Prakriti? Ishvarakrishna says in *Samkhya-karika* that Purusha without Prakriti is lame, whereas Prakriti without Purusha is blind. Purusha is lame because It cannot act without Prakriti. Is the ability to act unnecessary? Is action merely an appendage, or is it a necessary component of being human, or even of being divine? Can one imagine God without action? Why then are there descents of God to the Earth? Why then are there avataras? "If I were to cease working," says Krishna in the Bhagavad Gita "all these worlds would perish" (3:24). He advises his friend and disciple, Arjuna, to act on his own level and scale, as Krishna himself acts on the highest level and on the largest scale.

No teacher or tradition has ever suggested that there can be any spiritual understanding without a clarity of the mind and a cleansing of the perceptions. In the *Yoga Sutra,* in any case, there is much emphasis on physical and ethical preparation. Five of the eight limbs of Yoga speak of such preparation. The higher energy, even if it may descend by its own accord and according to its own will, still needs to flow into properly prepared channels. Otherwise the body and the mind can be deranged. It is understood in the practical schools of yoga that one needs to prepare the whole of the psychosomatic complex in order not only to *understand* truth, but also in order to *withstand* truth.

Far from wishing away the lower self, we need to cultivate it properly. In the Brihadaranyaka Upanishad, a self is asked for because it is necessary for Self-realization: "He created the mind, thinking 'let me have a self' ... the mind was set on the body. He desired, let this (body) of mine be fit for sacrifice and let me have a self (body) through this" (I.2.1–7). The same upanishad says, "Whoever knows thus, 'I am Brahman,' becomes this all. Even the gods cannot prevent his becoming thus, for he becomes their self" (I.4.10).

If we ignore the self, it will assert itself in myriad clever ways and express itself in fantasies about the Ultimate, quoting the sages and imagining that what has been heard has been understood and embodied. Self-consciousness, awareness of this self, is necessary as a part of sadhana. Self-realization is a consummation of self-consciousness. *Rita* (Order) and *satya* (Truth) are born from *tapas* (effort, austerity), as says the Rig Veda (X.190.1). If we remain anchored in the actual practice of yoga, in the search for conscience as well as consciousness, seeking oneness with all there is while being firmly grounded in our unique svabhava, then we may gradually be freed of the egoism of asmita. "In the state of freedom from asmita the resulting insight is naturally full of truth and order" (*Yoga Sutra* 1:48).

Teaching of Krishna, Master of Yoga

The Bhagavad Gita speaks about a wide range of levels, from the practical concerns of daily life to the highest realization possible for human beings. It is perhaps the most important single work to originate in India.

The basic setting of the Bhagavad Gita is a battlefield at Kurukshetra. In brief, the Kauravas and the Pandavas, who are cousins, are engaged in a battle to determine who would rule the kingdom. Krishna, who is God incarnate, had tried to stop the war, but the cousins could not come to any agreement. Both sides approached Krishna for his help in the conflict. He gave the opposing parties this choice: one side could have all his armies with their weapons, and the other side could have Krishna himself, but he would not carry any weapons in the war. Duryodhana, chief of the Kauravas, the sons of the blind king Dhritrashtra, had the first choice, and he opted for quantity; he chose the armies with all their weapons. Krishna, who would not take up weapons in the war, became the charioteer of Arjuna, the chief hero of the Pandavas. As the battle was about to start, Arjuna asked Krishna to take his chariot to a place in the middle of the two armies so that he could survey the warriors on both sides. When Arjuna saw that his own cousins, uncles, other relatives, and teachers were among the warriors he had to fight and he realized that he was about to enter into a battle with his own kin, he was bewildered about what the right response was.

In the middle of the most significant battle of his life, on the field of dharma (responsible action), Arjuna, a warrior by type and deep inclination, is confused about right action and about his responsibility. He sees that the different levels of dharma present conflicting demands. He turns to Krishna, now acting as his charioteer, for help and instruction. The Bhagavad Gita, which means "song of the Blessed One," contains the teaching given by Krishna to Arjuna, in this hour of his crisis of conscience and of conflicting dharmas.

It is clear right from the very beginning that the teaching is about dharma. In fact, the very first word in the Bhagavad Gita is 'dharma'. At the beginning, Arjuna is confused about dharma, but after receiving Krishna's teaching, he is clear about his responsibility. Dharma and the part we have in maintaining order at all scales is a central subject of the Bhagavad Gita. Sometimes, dharma is translated as 'duty'; this is partly right. However, it is closer to 'responsibility for the maintenance of order'. This is required at all scales: at the scale of the entire cosmos, of society, of the family, and of the individual. We are supported by the cosmos, by the society and by the family, but we need to support these as well.

It is useful to mention that Krishna and Arjuna, like most names in Indian mythology, have literal meanings. Krishna means 'black', and Arjuna means 'white'. Thus the Bhagavad Gita is a dialogue between the Dark Lord and the white pupil, between the Infinite and the finite, between the Unknown Mystery of the other shore and a wayfarer setting out from this shore, apprehensive and unsure. It is an exchange between different levels, within ourselves as well as outside. Although, as a literary device, Krishna and Arjuna are personified, and they may have been real historical figures, we are in the presence of forces and realities that are not merely personal. They are definite and concrete, but they are not limited or merely localized historical particularities. Krishna himself says "From me is all this world" (BG 7:7) or "This whole cosmos is strung on me like pearls on a string" and "I reside in the heart of every being"(BG 13:2). In these and in similar expressions, Krishna indicates that he operates at the largest scale and at the highest level. Arjuna, on the other hand, is confused about his action in a particular situation, at a very different scale and level.

The general outlook of the Bhagavad Gita is that every action, even the smallest, has a cosmic background and a cosmic effect, even though we may not be aware of this. It can, in fact, be really understood only if we see the whole picture and our proper place in it. There is a clear enunciation from Krishna that Arjuna should do on his own scale what

Krishna does on the largest scale. The idea that a human being has the possibility—not the actuality but the possibility—of being a microcosmic image of the whole cosmos is an idea which is central to Indian thought. A human being is called a *kshudra brahmanda*, a small brahmanda, 'the little egg of the Vastness'. The whole universe is brahmanda (the egg of Brahman, the Vastness) and a human being is a small brahmanda. Arjuna must do on his human scale what Krishna does on a cosmic scale; that is, he must assume responsibility for the maintenance of order.

But what Krishna is able to do is not possible for Arjuna to do, even on his own scale, because Arjuna is an uneducated man, because he is prakrita. Only a sanskrita person can mirror the large cosmos. A prakrita person, an ordinary, natural person, is unable to do so. 'Prakrita' means 'natural', 'vulgar', 'common', 'uneducated', whereas 'sanskrita' means 'refined' and 'cultivated'. If Arjuna is to be able to do what Krishna does, he must engage in yajña.

Yajña is a difficult word to translate. Most often, it is rendered as 'sacrifice', which is one meaning of this word. The verbal root also means, for example, 'to worship', 'to adore', 'to honor', 'to consecrate'. But in the most ancient texts, and also in the Bhagavad Gita, it refers to the occasion, or the process, or the means for an exchange of substances between levels. The invocation of higher forces at the level of the *deva*s or gods, or a feeding of them, is yajña. It is only through yajña, sacrifice, that the gods are sustained in their task of maintaining the world-order. The whole universe is said to be created as a yajña which is thus 'sacrifice' in the original meaning of the word, namely, 'to make sacred'. Only through yajña does a human being come in contact with higher states of being, the deities. We cannot live without participating in the cosmic rite, the universal yajña, either as instruments or as victims. Through the voluntary undertaking of sacrifice, that is, through yajña, human beings can offer self-will as an oblation so that they may be used as instruments of the divine will through an identification with what is highest in themselves. Arjuna has only the following choice: he can be compelled by his own nature, by prakriti, to fight as a victim of the cosmic drama, or he can see the necessity to fight as an instrument of Krishna's purposes. The suffering of the loss of self-will is the necessary requirement for undertaking this yajña. As it is said in myths, where every internal state is personified, Yajña is the son of Ruchi (Wish) and Akuti (Will). Yajña was created at the same time as human beings were, in the beginning, and it is always required.

According to the Bhagavad Gita (3:14–16), "yajña (sacrifice) is the fruit of right action. The value of action is determined by the knowledge of the permanent values found in the Eternal Law, and this Law is the expression of the principle of indestructibility which manifests itself in the perpetual rite of sacrifice that is the universe. The one who does not take a willing part in this endless sacrifice is made of sin. Imprisoned by the senses, human existence is without a purpose."[1] Without yajña, without a sacrifice and an exchange of substances with higher levels, dharma, the maintenance of order, is not possible. But an exchange of substances is not possible for a person ordinarily, except in the sense of mechanical nature, prakriti, in which everyone participates as a victim. In order for this exchange to be an intentional undertaking, one must be sanskrita; and in order to be sanskrita, one must be transformed.

This is where yoga, which is the discipline, path, or way to link levels is required. An ordinary person, who is prakrita, becomes sanskrita through yoga. In short, dharma is not possible without yajña and yajña is not possible without yoga. Therefore, Krishna has to teach Arjuna yoga in order to prepare him, to educate him, and to transform him so that he may become an intentional link between levels and scales.

The fundamental notion in the Bhagavad Gita, about how one can be educated, revolves around the idea of svabhava. This word means something like 'one's own becoming'. Sometimes, it is rendered as 'own being', or 'essential nature', or 'inborn nature'. Krishna himself, the spiritual element, resides in every person as svabhava. It is for the sake of fulfilling the purposes of svabhava that a person takes on a human incarnation. One would not say that the body has acquired a spirit; one would say rather that the spirit has acquired a body. The spirit takes on a body because it needs to do something, and if it does not do it before the death of the body, then it will have to be reborn again, and if necessary, again and again, at the same level, until it does what it must do. What a person is required to do is to fulfill svadharma, that is, dharma corresponding to svabhava. If a person accomplishes what is required, then the person, or the spirit, is freed from that level of existence and the corresponding manifestation. Then it may be able to undertake the demands of a higher level and it will be born accordingly.

Throughout Indian thought, and certainly in the Bhagavad Gita, it is said that the manifestation of one's svabhava depends on deep tendencies that are inborn and that are colored by the astral and the planetary influences at the moment of birth. The word that is used for what we call 'caste' literally means 'color' (*varna*). At the time of birth a certain major color or shade is impressed on the person in accordance with the state of the cosmos at that moment, giving a certain coloration to the deep tendencies which will be expressed throughout one's life. Thus each person starts with a certain cast of mind, a certain color of feelings, and some characteristic tendencies right from birth. Traditionally there are four main types of svabhava: brahmin (teachers, scholars, researchers), kshatriya (rulers, nobility, warriors), vaishya (bourgeoisie, especially business people and producers), and shudra (workers, proletariat). These castes do not depend on the caste of the parents. For example, a brahmin father could have a shudra son, or vice versa. However, for centuries in India, the parents' caste has, for social purposes, determined the caste of the children and the original insight about different types has become distorted.

There is another division that refers to the quality of response to one's congenital tendencies and essential calling. These qualities are divided into three major areas, the three gunas. One of them, for example, is tamas (carelessness). One may be a brahmin by essential calling, but a careless brahmin. One can be an active but agitated (rajas) brahmin, or one can be satva (aware and calm). Similarly, one can be an aware and alert shudra—a conscious laborer. Brother Lawrence would be a good historical example of a sattvic shudra, who served by his labors as a breadmaker while engaged in the practice of the presence of God. Similarly, Plotinus, Solomon, and Matthew may possibly serve as historical illustrations of a brahmin, a kshatriya and a vaishya whose responses to their inherent diverse callings were characterized by the quality of mindfulness. There are three main qualities of response to the four major inherent tendencies; thus we get twelve different kinds of human beings. Traditionally, it is recognized that shudras who are mindful of their own tasks and in their own work, are superior to those brahmins who are inattentive, heedless, or careless about their work. In any case, the quality of response is something quite different from the tendency or the calling to which one responds.

The Bhagavad Gita emphasizes that we cannot really be free without following our own svabhava, our own essential becoming. Corresponding to svabhava is svadharma, and also svakarma, work corresponding to svabhava. Only those actions and those responsibilities which correspond to our innermost tendencies and our proper place can lead to freedom. Of course, this freedom is only from a particular level of existence, and it will be realized only when the demands of that level are fulfilled. Otherwise, as Krishna says, we are compelled to return again and again to our own deep unsatisfied yearnings, which furthermore can be fulfilled only through our own essential calling. For example, when Arjuna says, "I shall not fight," Krishna replies (BG 18:59–61), "You say you will not fight, but you will come back to the battleground. Your way is that of a warrior. It is in your inherent nature. You cannot run away; something in you will compel you to fight. The Lord sits in the heart of every creature, making each revolve by his power as if mounted on a machine." Svabhava is the very particle of Krishna that is situated in every being, and it is only through that part that one can come to Krishna's own being. To come to Krishna—that is, to be and to act in his mode of being—is the ideal which is set out in the Bhagavad Gita. Svabhava is the vehicle for this. To come to Krishna, to this level of vast energy, is possible only through one's own essential nature, through svabhava. Krishna says (BG 18:45–48) that however difficult our svadharma is, that is, however hard the dharma corresponding to our svabhava is, however difficult our calling and duties are, and however pleasant or rewarding other people's ways appear, we cannot follow the dictates of any svabhava other than our own. There is no way to real freedom except through our own deepest and most essential nature.

The fundamental way that Krishna outlines in the Bhagavad Gita, that is to say, the fundamental yoga that he teaches Arjuna for transformation is buddhi yoga. This teaching speaks of the need for the integration of buddhi. Buddhi, the same word from which Buddha is derived, comes from the verbal root *budh*, meaning 'to wake up' or 'to discern'. Buddhi is the faculty of vision and of discernment and it is above manas, the mind. In an uneducated prakrita person, the desire-will—which arises mostly from the senses, likes-dislikes, pleasures and fears—controls the mind, which in its turn controls buddhi and dissipates it into conflicting desires. If a person is transformed, there is a reversal of this natural order, establishing the right internal order, which is a prerequisite for the maintenance of an external order. External dharma is possible only after the right internal order is established, and this is possible only through yoga. In the right order, buddhi controls the mind, which in turn controls the senses. Then buddhi receives its impulses and energy from something which is above it. This latter is called by many names. Krishna sometimes simply calls it 'that', or 'the embodied', or sometimes purusha or atman. Buddhi is the highest aspect of a specific individuality, and marks the divide between what is personal and something which is beyond the personal. Only buddhi is able to receive this higher vision; nothing else in a human being is able to directly receive it. If buddhi is not functioning properly, the attention is many-branched and disintegrated.

The purpose of yoga is to integrate a person. The word yukta means; 'one who is in yoga' or 'one who is integrated'. Buddhi yoga has several aspects to it, as a symphony orchestra has various musical instruments which are called upon to play in turn or together. Specific yogas, such as karma yoga, bhakti yoga, and jñana yoga, are the various musical instruments in this orchestra of buddhi yoga. Karma yoga means the discipline of action or integration through activity. Bhakti yoga is integration through love or devotion; jñana yoga leads to an integration through knowledge, through gnosis. Dhyana yoga is the yoga of meditation. (Ch'an in Chinese, Thon in Vietnamese, Son in Korean, Zen in Japanese are all variations on the Sanskrit dhyana. The practices of meditation in these different settings have all been influenced by dhyana yoga.) These yogas together constitute the buddhi yoga of the Bhagavad Gita, that is, the yoga of integrated intelligence and will.

Karma yoga is the yoga of action. It is the way of activity connected with the body and of all physical labor, of the arts and the crafts, of gestures, postures, and rituals. There are some fundamental aspects of the yoga of action in the Bhagavad Gita. The first is that we cannot be free of the bondage of action, that is, free of compulsive mechanical action, by inaction. When Arjuna saw the situation on the battlefield at the beginning of the Bhagavad Gita, he realized that he was not clear about right action and he wished to withdraw from action altogether. But Krishna reminded Arjuna that no one can refrain from acting while they live. The first renunciation Krishna asks for is the renunciation of inaction. The whole of life is a field of action and we cannot avoid responsibility for our actions. The second aspect connected with karma yoga is the requirement for the renunciation of attachment to any specific kind of activity and to the fruits of action. We must do what needs to be done, whether we like it or not, without anxiety about the success or the failure of the undertaking. Krishna also says that the only action that has the possibility of leading to freedom is yajña karma, activities done as sacrifice, made sacred by an exchange with higher levels. Krishna says that he himself is "the primordial sacrifice (*adhiyajña*) here in this body" (BG 8:4), and that it is out of yajña that the world was created. "By actions done other than for yajña, the world is bound; therefore, act without attachment" (BG 3:9).

Bhakti yoga is the way of feeling and of love and devotion. This is the yoga of the heart, of poetry, music, worship, and self-surrender. Krishna places much emphasis on the fact that all ordinary existence is controlled by raga dvesha, by like and dislike. Only one who is freed of the duality of like and dislike can see clearly and impartially. This is further elaborated in the terms of fear and pleasure, but the words used most frequently are raga dvesha, attachment and aversion, like and dislike. The possibility of any higher feelings, like love, compassion, or faith, can arise only when we are not consumed by the more subjective emotions. Bhakti yoga opens the possibility of a relationship of love and devotion with higher or with deeper aspects of external and internal reality. The love for that which calls from above, which is the same as from deep within, is an essential component of coming to know the deeper and higher aspects of ourselves and the cosmos. We must love Krishna, which is each person's most intimate self, in order to come to Krishna. It is said that only when we love something do we have the possibility of really knowing it. "By love a yogi comes to know Me, and what I am in essence; having thus known Me, he enters into Me" (BG 18:55).

Jñana yoga is the way of knowledge and discernment. It is the path of the intellect, of inquiry, of science and philosophy. The knowledge that is spoken of here is not information but insight, not the discursive knowledge of manas (the lower mind) but the transformational gnosis of buddhi (the higher mind), by which we participate in the essential nature of what we know. Thus to know Krishna is to become one with him in his mode of being. This knowledge is neither objective nor subjective, but it is knowledge of both the cosmos and the self. As Krishna, who is "the knower of the field in all fields," says, "True knowledge is [simultaneously] the knowledge of the field and of the knower of the field" (BG 13:2).

This knowledge, or rather this vision, is vouchsafed to us in contemplation and absorption when our psyche is in samadhi (perfectly composed and integrated) by dhyana yoga (the path of meditation). There is not much direct instruction in the Bhagavad Gita about this path, except the general suggestion of following the middle path in matters of food, sleep, and exertion. The need for the right attitude, physically as well as emotionally and intellectually, is pointed out. When our body, mind, heart, and breath are properly harmonized, and our attention is steady, our buddhi is said to be one-pointed and integrated.

The various yogas are all limbs of buddhi yoga, the way of an awakened and integrated intelligence and will. These yogas are not exclusive; they interpenetrate, supporting each other so that buddhi may receive from above and act below. Thus integrated, a person can engage properly in yajña, in the necessary exchange of substances, and become an intelligent link between heaven and earth. Becoming a microcosm, we can carry out the proper dharma which can support the right order. At the end of the Bhagavad Gita, when the teaching is completed, Krishna says, "I have taught you the profoundest knowledge; reflect upon it, without leaving anything out, then act as you wish." (BG 18:63). Arjuna is now a transformed man, awakened to his real situation, to his proper place, and to the necessity of action which is demanded of him. In fact, he no longer has any choice: he sees what must be done, whether he likes it or not, and he, as a yogi warrior, bends all his parts to that purpose. He says simply: "My confusion is ended; I have recollected myself through your grace; here I stand firmly, without doubt; I will heed your word" (BG 18:73).

To close this very brief introduction to the teaching of Krishna, Master of Yoga, let me end with a verse from the Bhagavad Gita (3:30):

Renouncing all actions to Me,
Mindful of your deepest self,
Without expectation, without self-occupation,
Struggle without agitation.

1 *The translation of these particular verses is adapted from Alain Danielou,* Hindu Polytheism *(New York: Pantheon, 1964) p 68.*

Dimensions of the Self: *Buddhi* in the Bhagavad Gita

The Bhagavad Gita is the most important text in the smriti tradition of India. This is the literature which is traditionally known and is remembered, as distinct from the shruti literature which is considered to be ultimately authoritative because it consists of what has been revealed or heard directly from a higher level. The Bhagavad Gita has been assigned a date some time from the fifth century BCE to the second century BCE. The Indian religious tradition, which is more interested in mythical truth than historical fact, places the Bhagavad Gita at the end of the third age of the present cycle of the universe and the beginning of the fourth, in the Kali Yuga to which we belong.

The Bhagavad Gita opens on the battleground of dharma (order, law, duty, righteousness) which is concretized at an instance of time at Kurukshetra. Krishna had earlier attempted to reconcile the Pandavas and the Kauravas, two feuding families of cousins. However, when war appeared inevitable, both sides wanted his help. Krishna proposed that one side could have all his armies with their weapons, and the other could have him without any weapons. The Kaurava chief, Duryodhana, had the first choice. In choosing the armies he showed little discrimination and intelligence, and no understanding of the true nature of Krishna. Arjuna rightly calls Duryodhana *durbuddhi* (BG 1.23), one whose buddhi is bad. The Pandavas were overjoyed to have Krishna on their side, for he is no ordinary man; as he declared himself later, he is the Supreme Person who pervades and sustains all the worlds (BG 15.17–19). Krishna became the charioteer of the greatest Pandava warrior, Arjuna, for the duration of the battle.

Before the actual fighting began, Arjuna asked Krishna to take his chariot into the middle of the two armies so he could survey all the assembled warriors. From there he sees his teachers, brothers, uncles, cousins, sons and other relatives and friends on both sides, ready to kill and be killed. Seeing this, Arjuna is bewildered about right action and, in despair, he turns to Krishna for guidance. Krishna's instruction, in response to Arjuna's need, is not only about this particular situation at Kurukshetra, but about dharma in general; hence about the end of dharma, namely, moksha, unconditioned freedom and Krishna's own mode of being, as well as about the paths by which Arjuna's being may be transformed so that it may draw closer to Krishna's. Krishna places Arjuna's specific situation in a larger context, viewing it from above, as it were, suggesting that every situation has cosmological foundations and every act has universal implications. The dialogue between Arjuna and Krishna is about dharma, as Krishna himself says at the end (BG 18.70).

Buddhi in the Bhagavad Gita

As was said earlier, the place of buddhi in the Bhagavad Gita is central. Krishna advises Arjuna to "seek refuge in the buddhi" (BG 2.49). "To them who are constantly integrated, worshiping me with love, I give that buddhi yoga by which they may draw near to me" (BG 10.10). Later, in the process of summing up his entire teaching, Krishna says again, "Renouncing mentally all actions to me, making me your goal, relying on buddhi yoga, become constantly mindful of me. Mindful of me, you will overcome all obstacles by my grace. But if because of self-centeredness you will not listen, you will perish" (BG 18.57–58).

What is this buddhi yoga, the path of buddhi, that leads to Krishna? It is both the integration of the buddhi and an integration by the buddhi in a mutually supportive evolution. Furthermore, it leads to the self-transcendence of buddhi.

Buddhi is derived from the root *budh,* meaning 'to wake up', which refers to a growing discernment, an awakening, and a realization. In the Bhagavad Gita, buddhi is distinguished from manas, which is the faculty of thinking. Manas stands in a hierarchical order of subtlety and priority between the senses and buddhi. Manas is fickle, unsteady, impetuous, and difficult to control—as difficult as the wind (BG 3.42; 6.34). It can, however, be controlled and brought to rest in the self by buddhi, by arresting and reversing the usual order, which is quite lawful and corresponds with Krishna's lower nature.

Ordinarily, the senses are drawn outward by the sense-objects, and manas follows them. The attachment of the senses to objects of pleasure gives rise to desire, desire gives rise to anger, anger leads to bewilderment, and this causes the mind to wander. A lack of steadiness in the mind in turn results in the deterioration of buddhi. Once buddhi is destroyed, a person is lost. Without purpose there is a dispersion of buddhi into many branches, for only a resolute buddhi is integrated (BG 2.41, 62, 63).

One who would follow the spiritual path should draw in the senses, as a tortoise draws in its limbs, and renounce samkalpa (imagination, inclination). Without the renunciation of samkalpa, no one can be free of desires, which have their origin in samkalpa. Free of desire, the senses can be controlled by manas. Manas can, in its turn, be slowly anchored in the self by buddhi if buddhi is established with steadfastness. When buddhi governs the mind from above in the right internal order, it has a quickness which can bring the unsteady mind, driven hither and thither by *rajaguna*, the passion principle in nature, back to stillness in the self. Such a yogi, whose mind is stilled and who is free of blemish, joins Krishna's higher nature and enjoys the highest bliss (BG 6.2, 24–27).

The initial integration which is required, according to the Bhagavad Gita, consists in the unification of buddhi. For this purpose, three renunciations are recommended. The first is the renunciation of inaction, which Arjuna is inclined toward in the beginning. Krishna himself says that although he needs to do nothing, he is constantly engaged in action; and if he were to stop working, all the worlds would perish. The second renunciation required is the renunciation of attachment to the fruits of action. Offering all actions to Krishna, one must do what needs to be done in order to sustain the world, as sacrifice and worship (yajña), understanding the principle of reciprocal maintenance between gods and human beings (BG 3.11–12, 19–25).

The third renunciation is the renunciation of samkalpa, imagination and desire-will. "The wise consider it to be renunciation: to give up works dictated by desire" (BG 18.2).

Corresponding to these three renunciations, three definitions of yoga are given in the Bhagavad Gita, indicating three different instructions for and stages of transformation. Yoga is skill in action, it is equanimity in failure and success, and it is breaking the connection with dukkha (suffering), the connection that is forged by desire and imagination (BG 2.48, 50; 6.23–24).

Works done according to yoga, in accordance with the above interior renunciations, will gradually lead to a weakening of the sense of egoism and of the craving for physical or psychological acquisitions. Then the buddhi can emerge as unified, attuned to the higher self (atman), and in samadhi, instead of being dispersed in multiple wishes and projects. This integrated buddhi is now able to bring about a proper and a harmonious functioning of the whole of the psychosomatic organism, effecting a second integration of the buddhi yoga.

According to the Bhagavad Gita, buddhi is a faculty that needs to be trained, purified, and unified. It can then bring about the integration of the whole of the self, body, heart, and mind. This faculty alone, which functions rightly only when educated by yoga, can have higher knowledge (jñana, as distinct from *vidya*, which generally means mental knowledge), higher feelings (such as shraddha or faith, and bhakti, which is love and dedication) and higher will (as contrasted with desire-will). Buddhi is thus the discriminative intellect that perceives correctly and acts accordingly; it is the intelligent and sensitive will that can act in harmony with dharma. In the Bhagavad Gita, right action and right knowledge are inseparable.

The really important function of buddhi in the Bhagavad Gita is to provide a link between what is higher and what is lower. It is a crucial agent in the transformation of being (*bhavana*). The whole process of development is demonstrated by Arjuna, who is called *kapidhvaja*, one whose banner is a monkey (BG 1.20). In the first chapter, Arjuna is deeply despondent and assailed by many doubts. He is paralyzed, overcome by pity and self-pity. He is confused about dharma, and refuses to fight. In the last chapter, his confusion is destroyed, his doubts are dispelled and he has recollected himself (BG 18.73). He is now a different person; he sees, understands and acts differently. Realizing his own and Krishna's true nature, Arjuna takes refuge in Krishna and does what needs to be done.

Krishna declares the five gross elements, corresponding to the five senses in the human microcosmos, as well as mind (manas), ego (*ahamkara*), and buddhi to be the eight components of his lower nature. Beyond this is his higher nature, the source of life by which the whole cosmos is supported. A part of his higher nature is Brahman, which in an individual is called the essential nature or inner being (svabhava). By itself Brahman is neither being nor not-being. Within all beings, it also contains them; although undivided it appears as divided among beings. This higher nature is more or less equated with purusha (person), as distinct from prakriti, which refers to Krishna's lower nature. Purusha is not bound by the three fundamental qualities (gunas) of prakriti, namely, satva (beingness, affirmation, light), rajas (passion, activity), and tamas (passivity, resistance, darkness) (BG 7.4–5; 8.3; 13.12–23). In addition to the ordinary meaning of purusha as person, there are three distinct kinds of purusha mentioned in the Gita (15.16–19): the perishable purusha, the imperishable purusha, and *purushottama*—highest purusha, who is other than both these and is also called *paramatma*, the supreme self. Krishna declares himself to be purushottama, which does not contradict him being the other purushas as well; they are also his and they are in him, but he is still beyond. Similarly, in addition to purusha, Brahman and atman, which refer to the constituents of the higher nature of Krishna, also have many divisions.

Prakriti and all its manifestations—such as the gross elements, senses, mind, ego, buddhi, thought, desire, hate, pleasure, and pain—are all together also called sharira (body) as well as *kshetra* (field), which is distinguished from *kshetrajña* (knower of the field). Krishna declares himself to be the knower of the field in every field. Then he says that true knowledge consists in knowing both the field and the knower of the field (BG 13.1–6).

We see that buddhi itself, although the highest part of any particular being, belongs to nature. Therefore, it is subject to the three gunas which, depending on which quality predominates, give it a different coloration. The buddhi which knows the distinction between activity and the cessation of activity, between right and wrong, between danger and security, between bondage and freedom is satvic; the buddhi which is unclear about these and understands them incorrectly is rajasic; and the buddhi which reverses reality is tamasic (BG 18.29–32).

However, although buddhi itself is a part of the lower nature, it is only through purified buddhi that one can go beyond prakriti. The function of yoga is to reverse the usual order of the emanations of prakriti. By following the path of yoga, the sensual person, at the periphery of the expanding circle of emanations (pravritti), moves inward to live from the buddhi. For this purpose Krishna advises the use of karma (action, work, deed), the chief creative force of prakriti, responsible for giving rise to different states of beings. Rather than renouncing karma, the generative force of prakriti can be used to move beyond prakriti itself by an interiorization of the renunciation of karma and by offering the fruits of karma to Krishna. Moksha can thus be approached through karma (BG 3.31; 8.3).

It is as if the circle of eternity and the circle of time almost touch each other in buddhi, but not quite. Well-honed and purified buddhi functions as the antenna for receiving messages from the other shore; it acts as a lookout into the nonpersonal spiritual dimension of atman-purusha-Brahman and as the guiding will of the individualized prakriti.

Krishna reminds Arjuna that prakriti is also a part of Krishna, and that it operates by his own creative and magical power (maya), although it does not constrain and limit him. Krishna urges Arjuna to fight and to do his part in the cosmic drama; he tells him that he must become an instrument of Krishna's purposes. Taking his stand in his own deepest nature, he should act without attachment. Renouncing all works to Krishna, self-recollected, without expectation, without acquisition, and without agitation, Arjuna can help to bring the right order into the world (BG 3.25, 30; 11.32–33; 14.12).

Although the Bhagavad Gita is concerned with what is beyond prakriti and therefore beyond action and becoming, work is necessary. Inaction cannot lead to freedom from the bondage of action. Action according to one's dharma, based on one's own essential nature (svabhava), carried out as a sacrifice is emphasized. The attempt to wake up to the indwelling svabhava and to act out the law of the inner being of one's svadharma must be made with a resolute and a quiet mind, without self-pity or self-importance. Arjuna's way is that of a warrior, and he is required to fulfill his svadharma and not someone else's.

Above the level of the purified buddhi, movement is in a wholly different dimension. In the state in which the senses are quieted and thought ceases, one can experience the boundless joy of the transcendent realm of atman. This joy cannot be perceived by any of the senses or by the mind, but only by buddhi. Having seen and overcome the process of emanation, the yogi stands stilled in Brahman, attaining to the sight of Brahman in which all beings and all things can be seen without attachment. Beyond all dualities and without a sense of ego or possession, a yogi is not anything or anyone in particular, for the individual being (svabhava) is merged with Krishna's being (*madbhava*). Such a one is no longer reborn as this or that (BG 6.20–25; 14.19–26).

Having led to Brahman, the task of buddhi yoga is essentially finished. It has made possible jñana of the transcendent realm. It has done so by a creative synthesis and balancing of four distinct, yet interdependent, yogas. The path of action or karma yoga, the path of love or bhakti yoga, the path of meditation or dhyana yoga, and the path of knowledge or jñana yoga constitute the four limbs of buddhi, which integrates them into an organic whole. Each of these yogas is taught and emphasized in its place, without losing sight of the others.

The various Indian schools of religious thought and practice, before, after, and contemporaneous with the Bhagavad Gita, seem to have shown a distinct preference for one or other of these yogas. In the process they usually become one-sided and lose the wholeness of spiritual life and the organic balance and necessary tension characteristic of the Bhagavad Gita. Krishna himself says that he taught his eternal yoga, a teaching of the supreme mystery, to Vivasvat, the sun god, who taught it to Manu, the first among humans. Taught from one to another, this yoga was known by sage-kings; but with the lapse of time this teaching was lost on earth (BG 4.1–3). Krishna then taught this yoga to Arjuna. Much sensitivity and care are needed lest this be lost again and again in partiality.

The unformed Arjuna, like linear thinkers before and after him, is anxious to have Krishna tell him one definite and clear path, clear to his untrained (*akrita*) and ordinary mind. Krishna, however, is less intent on giving Arjuna a one-dimensional, logical consistency or mental clarity. He plays a veritable symphony of yogas, and uses wisdom, tact, love, and terrifying form to help Arjuna become attuned to a higher wisdom. This higher wisdom is not of a personal intelligence, although it is within him. Nor is this jñana any mere speculative theory. The characteristics of jñana include absence of pride, nonviolence, patience, self-control, lack of identification with the ego-I, unfailing love-and-dedication to Krishna, and constancy in the knowledge of self (BG 13.7–11). Jñana is a way of life; it is a yoga. One who follows the yoga of knowledge lives this way. All other yogas complement and aid this one, just as it complements them.

Krishna himself is still beyond. He is the foundation of imperishable Brahman, of eternal dharma, and of absolute bliss (BG 14.27). He declares: "Having become Brahman, with tranquil self, a person neither grieves nor longs; regarding all beings alike he attains the highest dedication (bhakti) to me. By love and dedication he comes to know me as I really am, how great I am and who I am in truth; then knowing me as I am, he enters me forthwith" (BG 18.54–55). A person becomes Brahman, though it has always been so. Seeing or realizing Brahman is the same as becoming Brahman.

Sacrifice and Order: Yoga, Rita, and Yajña

Rita, the underlying universal order, has significance at the cosmological, societal, and individual scales, and at all levels of existence, as does dharma, which essentially supplants it in the post-Vedic Sanskrit literature. Even though rita gives birth to yajña (the sacrifice and exchange of energies between levels) only yajña permits the transformation of human consciousness and conscience for the purpose of reestablishment of rita, both internally and externally. As the *Yoga Sutra* says, only a transformed person has the insight which is naturally full of rita (YS 1.48).

A Mystery Am I

I know not clearly whether I am the same as this Cosmos:
A mystery am I, yet conceited in mind I wander.
When the first-born principle of rita entered in me,
Then of this Vak *(Logos) I obtained a portion.*
—*Rig Veda I,164,37*

Thus speaks the great sage Dirghatamas in one of the most striking verses of the Asya Vamiya Hymn of the Rig Veda in his thousand-syllabled speech (*sahasram vachah*) about the mystery of the relationship between *aham* and *idam*, between the I and the cosmos.

Both aham and idam are born of rita and are supported by it. The term 'rita' in the Rig Veda has many meanings—water, sacrifice, *aditya* or truth. It is the cosmic law governing the universe. The very existence and expansion of the earth and heaven depend upon rita. The Rig Veda says, "The whole universe is founded on Rita and moves in it" (IV,23,9). Rita is both all-pervading and transcendent. The Vedic rita is much like the ancient Chinese *Tao*, the Mother of all things, and as the *Tao Te Ching* says, "The Tao that can be spoken of is not the Eternal Tao." In the form of Vak, which is said to be the first-born of Rita (Rig Veda I,164,37), Rita is the Word, which was in the Beginning, was with God and was God, and apart from whom nothing came to be (John 1:1–3).

Though in its original intrinsic sense, rita transcends the power of space and time, the gods make it take the form of satya (truth) so that it can apply to the affairs of the universe. In some passages rita and satya are used as synonyms; as are their opposites, *anrita* and *asatya*—as in the phrase *Satyameva jayate nanritam*, "Truth alone triumphs, not untruth" (Mundaka Upanishad III.1.6). Also, it is said that Rita and Satya were born from Tapas (Rig Veda X,190,1), and are thus twins—coexistent and coeternal.

Moral law and obligation, which in later literature is increasingly conveyed by dharma, is contained in the notion of a more universal order of rita—even though in later Sanskrit, Rita is described as a child of Dharma. "Agni inflicts the severest punishment on those who commit transgressions against the law of Rita" (Rig Veda X,87,11). The gods are described as *ritvans* (the possessors of rita) as well as *rita vradhas* (those who bear the burden of carrying out *rita*). The gods arise in order to carry out the purposes of rita, and are called *ritajah* or *ritajatah* (those who are born of Rita). Gods are called *vratapas* because they carry out the *vrata* (vow) in obeying the law of Rita.

Rita and Yajña

As the gods must follow the law of rita, so should human beings. The preservation and maintenance of rita depends on the proper relation between earth and heaven (*dyava-prithvi*). This proper relation is based entirely on yajña by which alone an act or the whole life can be made sacred. 'Sacrifice' is derived from the Latin *sacre* + *facere*, which means 'to make sacred'. It is by yajña that one participates in the right order. Yajña is the 'abode of Rita', 'the home of Rita ', 'the dwelling of Rita' , or 'the path of Rita' (Rig Veda I,43,9; I,84,4; III,55,14). Yajña becomes the cause, the origin and the beginning of all righteous acts and it prescribes obligations of the world (Rig Veda I,164,50; X,90,16).

Yajña is the very navel of the universe (*vishva nabhi*); *ayam yajño bhuvanasya nabhih* (Rig Veda I,164,35). Yajña is the central thread binding together human souls with the souls of the gods, for everywhere and in everything "the all-pervading Brahman is ever established in yajña" (*sarvagatam brahman nityam yajñe pratishthitam*) (BG 3:15). Prajapati first fashioned yajña, and through it he wove into one fabric the warp and weft of the three worlds (Rig Veda I,164,33–35). Prajapati is also identified with Yajña. The creation is sustained through Yajña.

It is important to emphasize that yajña is not only sacrifice, in the sense that the lower levels must practice self-containment and obedience to what comes from above, but also it is the process of reciprocal exchange between levels. This is clearly brought out in the Bhagavad Gita where Krishna says: "Sustain the gods with yajña and let the gods sustain you, sustaining each other, you will reach the highest good. Fostered by yajña the gods will bestow on you the joys you cherish" (BG 3:9–16).

As in the Cosmos so in the Person

There is a universally understood traditional principle according to which kshudra brahmanda (microcosmos) essentially mirrors the whole *brahmanda* (megalocosmos or macrocosmos). What is cosmologically sung in the Rig Veda concerning yajña is specified for human beings' spiritual practice in the Bhagavad Gita and the *Yoga Sutra* of Patañjali. The *nabhi* (navel) of the cosmos is the *hridaya* (heart) of the person. Krishna, who is the very essence of yajña (*adhiyajña*, BG 8:4) in this body, is seated in the heart of everyone (*hrdi sarvasya dhishthitam*, BG 13: 17).

Krishna is seated in the heart of all of us as our svabhava, which is our essential calling or inner being. Only through being truly and deeply ourselves can we come to Krishna's being (madbhava). In order to carry out the actions and responsibilities corresponding to svabhava (svakarma and svadharma) a person needs to engage in yajña, sacrificing those parts of ourselves which do not wish to support the wishes of the deepest self. It is only *yajñakarma* which does not lead to the bondage of action. The way to be freed of the bondage—which is in fact the bondage of time and of causality—is not inaction, as Arjuna was tempted to think, but through an engagement in action carried out as a sacrifice and a sacrament. As Krishna says:

Renouncing all action on Me,
Mindful of your inner self
Without expectation, and without self-occupation,
Struggle without agitation. (BG 3:30)

However, yajñakarma is not possible for those who are prakrita (unformed, vulgar, uneducated) and who do what they like and wish for themselves. Only when they have been made sanskrita (cultured, well-formed, cultivated) by the discipline of a spiritual path, a yoga, are they inclined to and able to carry out the will of Krishna. In this transformed state, it is possible to be identified with the Highest—within the self and in the cosmos—which in the discourse of the Bhagavad Gita is labeled Krishna. There are no separate personal responsibilities when this takes place. As Krishna says:

Leave all responsibilities aside,
Turn only to Me as your sole refuge,
I will deliver you from all evil;
Do not fear. (BG 18:66)

Only at the very end of the transformation effected by the yoga of the Bhagavad Gita can Arjuna say that:

My confusion is destroyed,
I have remembered myself through your grace,
O Unshakable One, with doubts dispelled
I stand ready to do your bidding. (BG 18:73)

Yajña of the Mind

As a continuation of the Vedic sacrifice (yajña), the *Yoga Sutra* recommends the sacrifice of the limited and limiting mind (chitta) for the sake of purusha, who is the only true seer. This purusha is not personally yours or mine; it is the pure power of seeing. It is possible to sacrifice the limitation of the mind for the unlimited power to see. It is a sacrifice of the separated self—with all its fears and hopes, likes and dislikes, sorrows and pleasures, failures and ambitions—for the sake of the Only One who truly sees. Then the requirement of a sacrifice of the seen, for the sake of the Only One who truly is, follows. Then there is no separate object but purusha, there is no separate subject but purusha, there is no knowing but purusha. The seer, the seen, and the seeing are all One; there is no other. This is the state of kaivalya—of aloneness, not because there is an opposition or a separation but simply because there is no other.

In this fullness of being, in the vastness of reality, there is true order. In the *utsava* (festival) of life, all of sadhana (practice, effort) is yajña. In the movement from asmita ("I am this" or "I am that") to *Soham* (I AM), from a limited self to the Self, from the identification with chitta to one with Purusha, from the self-will of Arjuna to his willingness to carry out Krishna's will, the right order is discovered. The resulting insight is naturally full of truth and order (rita): *tatra prajña ritambhara* (*Yoga Sutra* 1:48–49; 2:15; 3:54). Sacrifice permits order. Yajña, born of Rita, is the ground for the reestablishment of Rita. As Shatapatha Brahmana says, "Yajña is the womb of Rita" (I.3.4.16).

Ahimsa, Transformation, and Ecology

Ahimsa and the Indian Tradition

It is an interesting paradox that on the one hand it can be said quite correctly that the highest ideal of a sage in India is *ahimsa*, while on the other hand, it does seem odd to associate ahimsa with the practice and symbols of Indian society, especially with the mainstream Hindu tradition. In his political activity Mahatma Gandhi popularized the common understanding of ahimsa as nonviolence and as refraining from hurting others, human beings and animals alike. Drawing inspiration mainly from Buddhist and Jain sources, he managed to give the impression that ahimsa is at the very heart of the Indian tradition. However, this popular understanding can hardly be derived from Hindu scriptures or mythology. Almost all Hindu gods and goddesses carry weapons, usually in more than two hands. They do so not just for adornment, for they use these weapons quite frequently, either to kill or to compel others to act in ways they would not otherwise act.

All the standard incarnations of Vishnu, especially the anthropomorphic ones—with the singular exception of the Buddha—engage in killing. The pictorial representations and descriptions of Kalki, the future avatara (incarnation) of Vishnu, inspire anything but thoughts of nonviolence. The Vedas, the two great epics Mahabharata and Ramayana, and the Puranas all depict and celebrate violence. Apparently Shankara, the great Advaitin, had a rule that anyone who lost to him in philosophical debate must commit suicide—a practice that could hardly be held up as a model of nonharming.

The Vedic sacrifices often involved ritual killing of animals. The Rig Veda (I,164,35) says that "Yajña (sacrifice) is the navel of the cosmos." To be sure, the Upanishads give a more internal interpretation of sacrifice (yajña)—see, for example, the opening verses of the Brihadaranyaka Upanishad—but that is not how it was understood during the Vedic times. Nor is the sacrifice during Durga Puja in a Kali Mandir without actual killing of animals. In Kashmir, a Brahmin must eat meat and fish at least during the festival of Shiva Ratri. It would seem that violence and killing have been one of the main features of the Indian society from the time of the Vedas until the present. Periodically, the killing is on such a vast scale—as with King Ashoka in the Kalinga battle—that the ideas of nonviolence seem appealing—temporarily.

Certainly, there is an invitation to ahimsa in India, and not only in Jain and Buddhist thought. When ahimsa is enjoined in the Hindu literature, as in the *Yoga Sutra*, it is for those aspirants (*sadhakas*) who are practicing withdrawal from the world (vairagya) and who are trying to engage in an order of existence that has laws different from the worldly ones. As long as we are active in the world, as Arjuna is exhorted to be by Krishna in the Bhagavad Gita, we are obliged to use carrot and stick (*dama* and *danda*), reward and punishment. Lakshmi, the goddess of wealth, is the power of Vishnu in his function as the preserver of order (dharma) in the world, and Arjuna helps Krishna in the destruction of the evildoers for the sake of upholding dharma.

Ahimsa is very subtle, both as an idea and in practice, and it does not always mean refraining from fighting or from hurting or even killing someone. Krishna advises Arjuna in the Bhagavad Gita to fight and to kill his enemies. Krishna is also known as Madhusudana (killer of Madhu) and Arisudana (killer of enemies); and Arjuna is called Parantapa (tormentor of enemies). Of course, the enemy may not necessarily be an external one. Yet the battle and the struggle inside requires a force, and is not only a matter of letting things be as they are. Internally or externally, there is no suggestion anywhere in Hindu literature to turn the other cheek when someone smites you. But Krishna says in the Bhagavad Gita (13:7 and 16:2, for example) that one of the characteristics of a wise person is ahimsa. Presumably, a wise person may kill someone while maintaining the practice of ahimsa. Is that so? Or is it not?

Ahimsa: Force and Violence

What is ahimsa? This word is almost always translated as nonviolence. This is not wrong, but it is partial; and partiality is itself a form of *himsa*, the opposite of ahimsa. Ahimsa means nonviolation and noninterference. This certainly includes nonviolence but is subtler and more comprehensive. In some cases, as in the Bhagavad Gita, ahimsa may require physical violence at one level in order to preserve what is regarded as more significant and inviolable. This is parallel to the necessity of transgression of one level of dharma by the demands of a higher dharma. During the war of the Mahabharata, Krishna advised Arjuna to override his sense of family dharma or societal dharma, or even his kshatriya (warrior) dharma, according to which he would not use treachery in killing his enemies even in the service of a higher vision revealed to him by Krishna.

It is necessary to distinguish between the use of violence and the use of force. It is not possible to be violent without using force, but it is possible to use force without being violent. If it were not so, all chastisement or disciplining by parents, teachers, or gods would be considered violent. Sentimentality would require that such disciplining be abandoned. However, every parent knows that children are not always amenable to rational discourse and persuasion, and need to be contacted at the level at which they can understand—including hugs and kisses as much as physical restraint. If one always adheres to the notion of not chastising children, it is unlikely that a sense of and need for inner discipline will find much place in the child for whose education one is responsible. It is possible that by sparing some physical pain earlier one would hurt the child more in the long run. If the great teacher Marpa had clung to the notion of ordinary nonviolence, the education of Milarepa at his hands would have been quite different. "Whoever I love, I reprove and chastise" (Revelation 3:19).

No action can be undertaken and nothing can be accomplished without energy, power, and force. Of course, the force might be that of persuasion rather than of physical violence, but that may not be effective. However, when all the wise counsel of the elders of the land, as well as all the vision and cunning of Krishna could not prevent the most disastrous war in the history of Bharata, there was nothing left but to fight physically. What could Arjuna accomplish without the use of his weapons and his skill in using them?

It is important to keep in mind a central idea of the Indian tradition, namely, that of levels. There is a hierarchy of levels within a person, in the society, and in the cosmos. The lower levels in all these are lower precisely because the level of insight and understanding there is not as subtle nor as comprehensive as it is at the higher levels. For example, those parts which are at a lower level in a person or in humanity wish to live by their own likes and dislikes and not by what is good or right for the whole person or the whole society. Those parts of us, or those among us, which understand the needs and requirements of the whole need to control, persuade, or coerce the lower parts to obey the higher vision. Otherwise, there will be chaos internally, in the society and in the cosmos, leading to a violation of right order (dharma) and of wholeness.

Once the idea of levels is understood, it becomes clear that the higher levels need to use force to control the lower levels. In order to gain an inner integration, there is an obvious place for the exercise of strength and determination in controlling the lower tendencies of the mind during the practice of yoga, or any other spiritual discipline. Even if we take the Bhagavad Gita completely allegorically, as speaking of the battle for the kingdom of the soul, we cannot escape the need for the use of force. All transformation needs force and energy, whether this transformation is an inner one or an external (technological) one. The use of force is violent when it does not serve the purposes of the higher levels. Ahimsa needs to be understood not in terms of appearances and external forms of conduct, but with regard to the internal intention and order involved. Egotistic intent and motivation, however placid, peaceful, and nonharming the external behavior may be, always carry seeds of violence in their very core.

Ahimsa in full measure is not possible for a person as long as the person is ego-centered. There are many relative levels of freedom from violence and manipulation. Ahimsa is not accomplished once for ever, and one needs to continually search for its dynamic source. Only at the highest level of being can one naturally manifest ahimsa; below that we can only approach it more or less. True ahimsa is a property of the real world, where it is a natural consequence of insight, as are compassion and love. To fix its understanding as nonharming at the level of the ordinary world is like taking sentimental love and attachment as the core of the Buddha's compassion. Giving an exclusive importance to physical harm, and not taking into account the mental, psychological and spiritual anguish caused by our actions, further strengthens the fallacy that a person is primarily a body, a fallacy that Krishna is at pains to dispel in the Bhagavad Gita.

Only a sage at the mountaintop sees the proper place of everything and everyone; such a person comes to a deep-seated acceptance of all there is. But all the sages who return to the world in order to be active in it and to teach others commend struggle—always internal and sometimes external. Perhaps it is only by an endless struggle between the higher energies of consciousness and the lower ones of forgetfulness that the play of forces, which constitute the cosmos, continues. A complete destruction of one side or the other would bring this play to a halt—a possibility only for the end of days when time shall be no more. Otherwise, as Krishna says in the Mahabharata, the choice is not between battle (*yuddha*) and absence of it, but only between one kind of battle or another. The real question then is at what level of existence and consciousness one is going to fight. As St. Paul says, "Finally then, find your strength in the Lord, in His mighty power. ... For our fight is not against human foes, but against cosmic powers, against the authorities and potentates of this dark world, against the superhuman forces of evil in the heavens" (Ephesians 6:10–12).

As the myths tell us, the Daityas and the Adityas are constantly engaged in a battle for the control of the cosmos. The Daityas, who are the children of what is limited (Diti) and of vision (Kashyap), and the Adityas, who are the products of what is vaster, unlimited (Aditi) and vision (Kashyap), are always naturally in conflict. The former are usually stronger at the lower level of brute force, and at that level are likely to physically overwhelm the subtler beings. The myth of the churning of the milky ocean is particularly striking and insightful. In this myth, the stronger half-brothers, the Daityas, who operate from a lower level, cannot be eliminated. Furthermore, they too are needed to assist with the churning of the milky ocean, the field of all that is, for amrita, the nectar of immortality. Later, after amrita has emerged, the Daityas are deprived of their share by cunning on the part of Vishnu, who succeeds owing to the inner weakness of the Daityas in the face of temptation. But cunning and strategy are as much instruments of manipulation as physical weapons are. And in this myth, when one of the Daityas, Rahu, becomes aware of the ruse of Vishnu and gets hold of amrita and starts drinking it, Vishnu uses his discus to cut his head off.

Transformation as a Human Imperative

What is the meaning of the Great Dance of Life in the cosmos? On a much smaller scale, what place do we human beings have in this Dance? First of all collectively: what role does humanity have in the cosmic economy? There are immensely vast stretches of time and of space, and humanity exists like an excrescence confined to a few meters' depth on the skin of the Earth. What is humanity in the midst of this immensity? No one can fail to appreciate the vastness, intricacy, and delicacy of the whole structure of the universe. The physical and chemical characteristics, not only of the environment on the Earth but also on the largest cosmological scale, seem to be so artfully and finely tuned, with humanity precariously balanced in a state of extreme fragility, that one cannot but endorse the cosmic feeling of awe which Einstein described as one of "rapturous amazement at the harmony of natural law."

It is a consequence of the amazing harmony of natural laws that human beings are here, that a hundred million of us die every year and a hundred million or more are born. We are not here contrary to law. We may not know the precise mechanism by which we came to be, and we may not know the function we have in the vast universe, but it is hard to imagine a scientist who does not see order in the universe, a pattern involving regularity of phenomena and generality of the laws and a harmony of the various forces which permit a continued existence and a constant unfolding of the world. The more we know about the universe, the more elegantly and wonderfully well-ordered it appears. Given the fundamental lawfulness of nature, according to which every creature and physical constellation has a function in the cosmic economy, we would expect that humanity also has a function and a role in the cosmos, even if we do not know what it is.

One can ask the question about the place of human beings in the lawful Dance of Nature, but this question is relevant on an individual scale also: What is my place? Why am I here? Am I completely replaceable in an ensemble of human beings as far as the vast cosmos is concerned? What meaning is there to my individual existence? What significance to my personal hopes and aspirations can there be? What was said several thousand years ago by a poet in the Rig Veda (I,164,37) can be said by any one of us: "What thing I am I do not know. I wander alone, burdened by my mind." This burden of the mind, this wandering alone in inquiry, this passion for knowing what one is and how one is related to the cosmos, is peculiarly human.

Human beings have the possibility of intentional action. What is fundamentally at issue is the possibility of transformation from one level of being to another. It is as though we are unfinished creatures as we are; and the world is incomplete and unfinished along with us. However well-balanced and ecologically sound the universe may be without our human interference, we seem driven by our deepest internal necessity, possibly in fulfillment of a requirement of the cosmos, not only to understand the cosmos but also to transform it. We cannot be human unless we intervene in the natural order both inside us as well as outside. Human beings are creatures who must intervene; they cannot leave themselves or the cosmos the way they find them.

Transformation is not just any change; it is intentional change; it is not natural, which is to say, it will not happen without intention. All works of art are examples of transformation. An intentional intervention is required to bring into existence a sculpture from a stone. We are constantly called to make ourselves, the earth, and the whole universe into works of art. In the transformation of a human being, great art and struggle are needed. If we are properly educated, we become able to be not wholly controlled by our natural inclinations, and we are able to intervene in our internal cosmos. Each one of us is an artist of our life: starting from the raw material of our own self, we sculpt something from it which corresponds to the level of our engagement, to our aspirations, our understanding, our skill, and our sensitivity. What we make of ourselves does not depend only on our own abilities and on our efforts but also on the various forces assisting or hindering us. But we must engage in the work of transformation; this is an imperative of our human existence.

Ecology and the Natural

One of the features associated with the ecological movement is a tendency to assume that science and technology are bad. Ecologists would much rather that nature be left alone in its wild and untransformed state. Transformation, on the other hand, is practically a human imperative, as we have seen. We need to be careful and to avoid the pitfalls that we can anticipate. The first difficulty lies in the use of the words 'nature' and 'natural'. In saying that transformation is not natural, I do not mean to suggest that it is artificial in the pejorative sense of that word. I more mean to say that it requires art and work and that it will not be done automatically or without intervention. Another way of saying this is that human beings have a purpose to their existence; they are needed in the cosmos. A human being fulfills this purpose when engaging in the work of inner and outer transformation.

We may distinguish purpose from function in the same way that transformation can be distinguished from change, namely, by the necessity of intentional intervention. Whatever our function in the scheme of nature, it will in any case be performed automatically in response to natural forces, as are the functions of kelp and lobsters. As we are born, breathe, procreate, and die, we fulfill our natural function, whatever it may be. The hundred million who die this year fulfill this natural function. But the fulfillment of our purpose needs an active participation on our part, a certain degree of choice and intention. This is what gives meaning and significance to our lives. Our function could be fulfilled collectively and interchangeably by one person or another; but the accomplishment of our purpose requires a unique engagement by each one of us. It is commonplace in many ancient traditions to speak in terms of the two natures of a human being, one concerned with purpose and the other occupied with function, often labeled 'higher nature' and 'lower nature', frequently in conflict with each other. The important point to be made here is that the human beings do not fulfill their purpose unless they engage in a struggle with their lower nature. Therefore, idioms and metaphors of battle, struggle, and fighting are practically universal in spiritual literature; the Bhagavad Gita provides the best example.

We cannot refrain from struggle without denying our higher nature. The real question is "What do we serve in this struggle?" Only those who serve the highest level can be completely free of violence, himsa. Quite typically in the Indian philosophical tradition, the highest resides in the deepest part of the person. The first and the most fundamental principle of ecology, therefore, requires an internal transformation so that there is a proper order, a wholeness and a lack of violence. Transformation, whether it is inner or outer, spiritual or technological, needs force (*virya*), power (*tejas*), determination, and steadfastness. Violence arises in the inversion of the right hierarchy: when an attempt is made to appropriate the higher in the service of the lower.

In the ancient world, a developed human being is understood to be a microcosmos that mirrors the large cosmos, and vice versa. A human being is a kshudra brahmanda modeled in all crucial aspects on the vast brahmanda. The person is not limited by the body, nor is the boundary between the inner and outer determined by the skin. As the Katha Upanishad (II.1.10) puts it, "What is within us is also without. What is without is also within. He who sees difference between what is within and what is without goes evermore from death to death." Internal violence, as well freedom from it, cannot help but reflect itself in the surrounding cosmos, and more particularly in close relationships. This is the lesson of all spiritual traditions, including the ones in India: we cannot be right with respect to external nature unless we are right with respect to our internal nature.

Inner (spiritual) and outer (technological) transformation is a human imperative, and all transformation needs force. Unless the transformation is undertaken as a service to the higher levels, for the sake of maintaining the right internal and external order, the force will lead to violence. It is important to emphasize that the real practice of ahimsa lies in a progressive freedom from the egotistic self and less in the external behavior. It is only in the light of the goal of completely selfless action that one can understand why the Indian tradition may hold ahimsa as the highest ideal and yet not refrain from carrying and wielding weapons for the maintenance of dharma.

The root of violence, both at the level of an individual and the society in the large, lies in partiality and in the denial of our wholeness. As long as there is the other, there is fear. Only when one realizes, as did Ramana Maharshi, who said "There are no others," can there be freedom from fear and consequently, from violence. Nonviolence (ahimsa) is a characteristic of a sage; for us it may serve as an invitation to practice, a step toward wholeness. The first principle of true ecology is ahimsa, primarily toward oneself. We need to know ourselves deeply, to suffer what we are and to accept ourselves. Then, a natural and right transformation comes about, a consequence of which is acceptance of others, male and female, foreigners and natives, of all creatures, and of the earth. In seeing ourselves impartially, we see others truly. From that seeing comes love.

Yoga and Other Paths

The Yoga of the Cross

As has been remarked earlier, yoga can refer to any path that relates the human soul with the Divine Spirit. The teaching of the Christ is a yoga par excellence for those who would follow the path of the cross. The following excerpts have been taken from *The Gospel of John in the Light of Indian Mysticism*, my study of the gospel that has been considered the most spiritual of the four canonical gospels.

Levels of Seeing

> *In spite of the many signs that Jesus had performed in their presence, they refused to believe in him. This was to fulfill the word of the prophet Isaiah: "Lord, who has believed what we have heard? To whom has the might of the Lord been revealed?" The reason they could not believe was that, as Isaiah said elsewhere, "He has blinded their eyes, and numbed their hearts, lest they should see with their eyes and comprehend with their hearts, and turn to me to heal them." Isaiah said this because he saw God's glory, and it was of Him that he spoke. There were many, even among the Sanhedrin, who believed in him; but they refused to admit it because of the Pharisees, for fear they may be ejected from the synagogue. They loved more the praise of men than the honor which comes from God. (John 12:37–43)*

It can be said that blindness to reality and the state of spiritual death are quite natural and universal, according to God's own laws. Even the devil cannot exist without God's consent and without ultimately serving God's purpose. From that point of view, spiritual awakening is against the current of God's own law of nature, or, as it is sometimes said—by Krishna, for example, in the Bhagavad Gita, or by Plotinus in the *Enneads*—that spiritual development is according to the higher human nature and is contrary to the lower nature. The power and glory of God are revealed only to a few, and what they hear is not heard or believed by the multitude, as the prophet Isaiah said. It is not that the masses do not wish to understand or believe, but that they cannot; or we may say that they understand only at the gross level and not very subtly. There is no question of any injustice here, any more than there is in remarking on the fact that a tiger can run faster than a human being but cannot think as well as an ordinary person. Within the general range of Homo sapiens there are many levels of spiritual development, and every tradition is thoroughly cognizant of this obvious fact of spiritual hierarchy.

Sometimes, of course, a person may be very struck and saddened by the unrealized potential of human beings and the general heaviness of humanity. Nevertheless, as is clear in the saying of Isaiah, it is God who has blinded the eyes of humanity and numbed their hearts so that they may not really see. The early Christians were so struck by the validity of this saying of Isaiah that each of the four Gospels reports it explicitly (John 12:40, Matthew 13:13–15) or implicitly (Mark 4:12, Luke 8:10); it is also to be found in St. Paul's Letter to the Romans (11:8), as well as in the Acts of the Apostles (28:26–27). Clearly it was well understood that it is quite in accordance with God's will and intention that the general masses should not comprehend any subtle truths, and therefore that they should not believe in Christ.

Furthermore, it was considered risky for the unprepared masses to be told higher truths, lest they misuse them for their egotistic purposes. Jesus Christ seems to have gone out of his way to ensure that even when the multitude heard him, they would not really understand. He said to his disciples, "To you the mystery of the kingdom of God has been confided. To the others outside it is all presented in parables, so that they will look intently and not see, listen carefully and not understand, lest perhaps they repent and be forgiven" (Mark 4:11–12), "for many are called, but few are chosen" (Matthew 22:14). From all this, we are forced to conclude that even when he spoke to large crowds, he did so only for the sake of the very few who were called by God to be able to hear him and see him with ears and eyes other than the gross ones. For the sake of these few, he suffered ridicule from the crowds and bore their stones. Finally, for their sake, he suffered crucifixion at the hands of the authorities who were afraid that he was inciting the crowds, whereas he himself had little interest in the crowds. In his last prayer to God, Jesus Christ said, "I have given you glory on earth by completing the work you gave me to do. ... I have made your name known to those you gave me out of the world. These men you gave me were yours; they have kept your Word" (John 17:4–6).

The basic question is of the right inner preparation for understanding spiritual truth, which is the same as believing in Christ. Without proper preparation of the recipient, truth can fall into the wrong hands and be misused, for as St. Paul said, "The Kingdom of God is not a matter of talk, but of power" (I Corinthians 4:20). The higher forces and the great teachers, who are seldom sentimentally compassionate, are therefore as interested in imparting the higher knowledge to the well-prepared and rightly deserving people as they are in hiding and guarding it from the unprepared and undeserving. This goes right back to the fall of Adam: "And the Lord God said, 'Behold, the man has become as one of us, knowing good and evil. He must not be allowed to put forth his hand and take also of the tree of life, and eat, and live for ever.' The Lord God therefore banished him from the garden of Eden, to till the ground from which he had been taken ... and He stationed the cherubim and the fiery revolving sword, to guard the way to the tree of life" (Genesis 3:22–24).

Even when we understand the truth, still more is needed for a wholehearted commitment to it of the kind shown by the close disciples of Jesus Christ, including Lazarus and Mary, so that we stake our all to follow it wherever it may lead. It is not easy to die to the overwhelming force of approval and disapproval of others. We can have nothing but sympathy for those members of the Sanhedrin, Nicodemus and Joseph of Arimathea for sure and perhaps others, who were able to recognize the quality of the being of Jesus Christ, even though the forces of human bondage were too strong for them to forsake all to follow Christ.

The Yoga of the Cross

> *Jesus proclaimed aloud: "Whoever believes in me is actually believing not in me but in Him who sent me. And whoever sees me is seeing Him who sent me. As Light have I come into the world so that no one who believes in me need remain in darkness. If anyone hears my words and does not keep them, I am not the one to condemn him; for I did not come to condemn the world but to save it. Whoever rejects me and does not accept my words already has his judge, namely, the word that I have spoken—that is what will condemn him on the last day, because it was not on my own that I spoke. No, the Father who sent me has Himself commanded me what to say and how to speak, and I know that his commandment is Eternal Life. So when I speak, I speak just as the Father told me." (John 12:44–50)*

As far as Jesus Christ is concerned, the right preparation consists in dying to self-will and in denying the self, so that a person can obey the will of God. His yoga consists of this, and the cross is the supreme symbol of this. Whether or not it corresponds to any actual method of killing Jesus, the enormous psychological and spiritual significance of the cross cannot be exaggerated. Every moment, whenever we are present to it, we are at a crossing; at this point of crossing we choose whether to remain in the horizontal plane of the world or to be yoked to the way of the Christ and follow the vertical axis of being.

The way of the cross consists in surrendering ourselves completely to the will of God and emptying ourselves of our self-importance. Jesus Christ himself sets an example of this, as we have seen many times already. He has become so transparent to the Ground of Being that anyone who sees him sees God. He has nothing of his own; he does not speak in his own name or on his own authority. To use an analogy given in the *Yoga*

Sutra, the mind and being of those who are truly liberated are like a perfectly polished clear diamond, without any blemish at all, so that the glory of God can be reflected as it is. The words and actions of the Father are transmitted then without any distortions introduced by the personal ego. Since the words of the liberated are not their own, to hear them is to hear God; not to accept them is to reject God, who alone is the judge.

It is important to remember that Jesus was a crucifer before his arrest and trial, which eventually led to his death by crucifixion. The way of Christ is that of the cross. As he repeatedly told his disciples (see Matthew 10:38, 16:24; Mark 8:34; Luke 9:23, 14:27), no person is worthy and capable of being his disciple unless he takes up his own cross—not only as an idea but also as a daily practice—and follows him. In the language of symbols, the only one appropriate to these realities—a fact not lost to the early Christians—crucifixion is the only just manner of death of the Crucifer. Naturally, he who is "the Light of the world" (John 8:12) must be born on the darkest day of the year, just as "the Lamb slain from the foundation of the world" (Revelation 13:8) should have been killed on the day appointed for sacrificing the paschal lamb. The actual historical facts follow from the mythic and symbolic necessity and truth of the incarnation and the crucifixion.

The way of the cross, like all authentic spiritual paths, demands human sacrifice. As the Gospel of Philip says, "God is a man-eater. For this reason men are sacrificed to Him" (II, 3:63). When we are emptied of our own self, we can be filled with God and become one with the source. Thus the end of a person is the end of the person. In the way of the cross, there is no place for egoistic ambitions and projects; as a Hasidic saying has it, "There is no room for God in him who is full of himself."

Those Who Love Can Come to Truth

> *"If you love me, you will keep my commandments. I will ask the Father and he will give you another guide [paraclete] to be with you forever: the Spirit of truth which the world cannot accept, because it does not see it or know it, but you do recognize it because it remains with you and*

> *is within you. I shall not leave you orphans: I am coming back to you. A little while now and the world will see me no more; but you see me as one who has life, and you will have life. On that day you will know that I am in my Father and you are in me and I in you. Whoever keeps the commandments that he has from me is the man who loves me; and the man who loves me will be loved by my Father, and I shall love him and reveal myself to him."*
>
> *Judas (not Judas Iscariot) said to him, "Lord, why is it that you will reveal yourself to us and not to the world?" Jesus answered, "If any one loves me, he will keep my word. Then my Father will love him, and we shall come to him and make him our abode. Whoever does not love me does not keep my words; yet the word you hear is not my own but is of the Father who sent me. This I have said to you while I stay with you. But the guide, the Holy Spirit, whom the Father will send in my name will instruct you in everything, and remind you of all that I told you." (John 14:15–26)*

There is a progressive spiral of dedication, action, and knowledge, or rather of love, obedience, and truth, along which Jesus has been preparing the disciples. Here it is explicitly stated that if the disciples love Christ, this love must be evident in the fact that they obey his commands. Only to such persons can truth be revealed. The more they know Christ, the more they are drawn to him; the more they love him, the more they try to act according to his instructions; and the more they obey him, the more they come to understand him. There is a very similar spiral movement in the Bhagavad Gita, where there is a subtle interplay between action (karma), love (bhakti), and knowledge (jñana), all under the guidance of the teaching of the integrated intelligence (buddhi yoga), each aspect supporting and furthering the other. The disciples are thus more and more prepared, until they can recognize and receive the Spirit of truth, which will dwell in them permanently. The Holy Spirit had descended on the head of Jesus, witnessed by John the Baptist, and stays, dwelling in him forever. Now, in due course, she will descend and dwell in the disciples. This is how Christ himself will come again and show himself to them spiritually and dwell in them. It is the Spirit that is eternal, and not the flesh. Of course the flesh of Jesus must die according to the laws of the flesh, but those who are prepared and open of heart can see and receive the Word, who will come and dwell in them, and then they will understand the subtle truths.

He will reveal himself to them this way precisely because they would have been readied by the practice of love, obedience, and knowledge, and no doubt further shaken into a state of emotional openness by the shock of the death of their master. The question asked by Judas can scarcely be other than a literary device for the author of the Gospel: Of course, the world cannot see or recognize the Spirit of truth; the world has not been prepared. As has been emphasized throughout the Gospel, the crowds cannot grasp anything subtle. Even the disciples can hardly understand what is being said much of the time, and this in spite of their long training at the hands of the master for whom they have given up their comforts, professions, families, social positions, and everything else. Are the disciples disheartened at the lack of discernible progress in their understanding? Do they feel themselves to be just like everyone else in the world? Or is it genuine humility on their part that they do not even realize their distinctive situation? In any case, spiritual development also has its rhythms and time, as does natural growth: However much water may be applied by the gardener, the fruit ripens only in its season. The hour of these disciples is not yet.

Those Who Have Nothing Will Not Die

> *"Peace is my farewell to you, my peace is my gift to you; I do not give it to you as the world gives peace. Do not let your hearts be troubled and do not be fearful. You have heard me tell you, 'I go away for a while, and I come back to you.' If you truly loved me you would rejoice that I am going to the Father, for the Father is greater than I. But now I have told you this even before it happens, so that when it takes*

> *place you may believe. I shall no longer speak with you, for the Prince of this world is coming. In me he has nothing; but the world may recognize that I love the Father, and I do exactly as the Father has commanded me. Rise up, let us go from here." (John 14:27–31)*

The peace of Christ is the consummation of all spiritual effort and struggle; it is coming to rest in oneness with the Vastness. But only those who have been denuded of themselves can find this peace, for his peace is not like the peace of the world. As he said earlier, he came to bring not peace but dissension, to bring a separation between those who are blind but wish to see and those who do not even realize that they are blind, between those who are asleep but seek to wake up and those who love their sleep. And above all, he came to bring this separation and struggle in the soul of his disciples so that their own more spiritual aspirations might be strengthened in the warfare against the parts that deny the Spirit. He did not come to bring comfort or ease or happiness in any usual sense. He brought, in the words of St. Paul, peace "that surpasseth all understanding" (Philippians 4:7). Only those who obey the law of Christ, and like him are willing to die to themselves, can love him and come to his peace.

The disciples do not have a clear and continuing understanding of the true nature of Christ; in that sense they do not yet believe. They do not realize that the really significant part of Christ cannot die when his body dies, and that the same is true for them as well. They need the assurance from Christ that he is in fact on his way to a higher and more exalted place, in the presence of the Father, and that they should not be distressed for his sake nor be fearful for themselves. As Krishna says in the Bhagavad Gita, "The unreal never is: the Real never is not. This truth indeed has been seen by those who can see what is true" (2:16). Most of the disciples do not quite see what is true. They do not realize deeply enough that the prince of this world has sway only on worldly things, on things of the flesh, and not on the things of the Spirit. Christ has so completely emptied himself of all the worldly things, which have ultimately to do with fear and desire, that as far as the prince of this world is concerned, Christ has nothing on which he can lay hold. Being free of himself, he is free of the rulers of the world.

Naturally, the body of Jesus will be killed according to the laws of the world; but this by no means puts an end to Christ. He took on a body in obedience to his Father; and he will leave it also in obedience to His will. This is how he manifests his love for God, as he has repeatedly said that those who would love him must obey his word. In the entire Bible this is the only place where Jesus says that he loves the Father. It is only right that he should affirm in the very next breath his total obedience, made even more striking in the context of his imminent death. Having completely denied his self-will, he becomes one with the Father and the source of eternal life; in doing His will he leaves nothing in himself for the prince of this world to take hold of. *Theologia Germanica* says: "If the Evil Spirit himself could come into true obedience, he would become an angel [of light] again, and all his sin and wickedness would be healed and blotted out and forgiven at once."

Uniqueness and Oneness in the Lion's Roar: Vedanta and the Sikh Yoga

The face of Truth is covered with a golden vase.
Uncover it, O Lord, that I who love the truth may see.
—*Isha Upanishad 15*

Among the many and varied yogas developed in India is the way elaborated by the great gurus of the Sikh tradition. Initiated by Guru Nanak (1469–1539), the path was further enhanced by ten gurus, culminating with the turn given by the tenth guru, Guru Gobind Singh (1666–1708). He gave the name Singh to all his male followers to indicate that they were 'lions' among men. Since his death, Guru Granth Sahib, the sacred book of the Sikhs, has been regarded as the living guru. The religion of the followers of the gurus, Sikhism, naturally shares many common principles with other religions of India.

It is important to emphasize that a vast majority of the adherents of any religion do not and cannot live according to the great principles and injunctions of their religion. These principles are enunciated by the sages or the founders of the religions based on their direct experience; they are founded on insights which come from on high and they are received on the mountaintop. These insights and visions are always received in special states of consciousness where the ordinary mind and the corresponding language do not operate. These sages, through their words and actions, act as beacons of light for those who would follow them and come to the mountaintop where they themselves could receive illumination directly from the Source. But most of us—almost all of us—whether we label ourselves Hindus, Sikhs, Buddhists, Christians, or whatever, are being driven by forces other than the wish to connect with the highest or deepest insights; we are driven by egotism, fear and desire. We also press the sayings of the sages and other forms of religion into the service of these negative forces.

In general, the history of religion is the saddest of all histories; religions have been the source of much terror and oppression. People of goodwill should not belong to any religion; they should attempt to belong only to God who does not belong to any religion. As Guru Nanak said, "There is no Hindu; there is no Muslim. There is only Man." It is true that for a few, very few, religions are also the source of compassion, freedom from selfish craving and of self-transcendence, and therein lies all the hope of humanity. These are the few in any religion we should listen to and emulate. We should always be wary of the officials, organizers, and politicians of religion. Organized religions are by their very nature idolatrous—worshiping a person, a myth, an image, a place, or a concept. These are precisely what the organized religions are organized around. Any of these worshiped objects may be of assistance in one's own journey to Truth; but one has to be constantly on guard. Symbols can so easily shroud, veil, and replace the very reality they are supposed to reveal. The finger that points to the moon can hide it if held too close to the eye! No rosaries, no genuflection, no repetitions of any mantra can substitute for a compassionate and a loving heart. As Kabir said:

Ages have passed turning the beads,
But turning of the heart has not occurred.
Put aside the beads of the hand,
And turn the beads of the heart.

All the sages call for this reorientation of the mind and the heart, rather than scriptural learning, execution of liturgical details, or doctrinal disputations. The movement in the new direction—away from selfishness and fear—imparts authority to the words of a sage. This authority is not ecclesiastical; it is a moral and spiritual authority—from lived experience, not from hearsay or reading. Kabir said:

Oh Scholar, you speak of what you've read;
What I say is what I see.

Jesus taught them "as one with authority, and not as the scribes do" (Matthew 7:29). He spoke of what he knew, and testified to what he had seen (John 3:11). Kabir again:

There is nothing but water at the holy bathing places;
and I know that they are useless, for I have bathed in them.
The images are all lifeless, they cannot speak;
I know, for I have cried aloud to them.
The Purana and the Koran are mere words;
Lifting up the curtain I have seen.
Kabir gives utterance to the words of experience;
And he knows very well that all other things are untrue.

We also need to be wary of the philosophers and theologians of any religion. These philosophers, theologians, and preachers use words but not "words of experience." In general, they have no authority for they have not "lifted up the curtain." They do not have the wisdom of the other shore; they merely run up and down this very shore, shouting slogans and trying to convert others, far too often in order to increase a sense of their own importance and security. If we had a right valuation of the sages, we would realize that they belong to a somewhat rare species. There are not, and perhaps cannot be, many sages or saints—in any culture or religion. Very few human beings experience the Highest Vision—of the Ultimate, of God, of Truth, of the Source or of the One. But for those who are blessed with such a vision, it overwhelms their own personality and ego, and fills them with something that they can neither contain nor ignore. They are driven to manifest and speak about That which is not theirs but which they cannot but obey. They do not know That, but That knows them and commands them to say what they say and do what they do. And even these sages cannot stay at the absolute peak of the mountain for very long. They have to come down, even to survive as human beings, and also no doubt in order to teach the rest of us to mend our ways and to radically reorient (metanoia) ourselves toward That.

It is to be expected that any theorizing based on the words articulated by the spiritual masters on or near the mountaintop, but elaborated by those—almost everybody, with very rare exceptions—who do not have the comprehensiveness or the intensity of the whole vision, is a further spinning of the webs of illusion and confusion. Philosophers and theologians cannot but add confusion by their theorizing, unless they are disciplined by the spiritual practice of freedom from ego, and remind themselves constantly of the limitations of their words and ideas. No wonder the Buddha, who woke up from the hypnotic sleep of self-occupation and selfishness—the mainstays of which are fear, desire, concepts, words, and ideas—and saw directly, said, "The Tathagata has no theories."

So, even as we ourselves philosophize, we wish to be mindful of what has been said above. It is said that among the Hindus and the Muslims, Guru Nanak preferred to associate with the wandering and poor yogis and Sufis who searched for God rather than with the established and influential pandits and mullahs who preached God. We may speculate as to whom he would have chosen today to represent his religion and that of his disciples, the Sikhs. Still, if the mind is in its right place, in the service of the One, it does not have to be taken in by its own hubris; it can bring us to clarity and to a recollection of the right path.

Vedanta and the Denial of Otherness

The greatest insight of Vedanta, the most influential school of Indian philosophy, is the oneness and the sacredness of all reality. This is especially strongly expressed in the Advaita Vedanta tradition of Shankara. There is only one reality, and that is Brahman; everything else—that is, anything which can be claimed to be separate from it—is false. In our own times, the contemporary Vedantist sage Ramana Maharshi often said, "There are no others." It is the otherness that the Vedantist denies. The *tremendum mysterium* of the *Totaliter Aliter* of the Abrahamic tradition, forcefully described by Rudolf Otto in *The Idea of the Holy*, cannot be satya (true, as well as real) in the last analysis, according to the Vedantist philosophy, for ultimately Brahman and Atman are identically one. Plurality may be allowed by a Vedantist, but only at a lower level of relative truth, of appearance, and of ignorance. Vedanta thus offers a classic case of ecumenism by condescension: the other is also right—after all, as the Rig Veda (I.164.46) says, "Reality is one; the wise speak of it in many ways"—but as long as the other wishes to be distinct, that person's ignorance is declared. In spite of the saying of the Rig Veda, and in spite of the insights of the great sages of India, most Vedantist philosophers would consider anyone wise unless that person spoke of reality only in one way! Not Gautama the Buddha, nor Jesus the Christ, nor Guru Nanak.

From a strict Vedantist point of view, the Sikh tradition, as much as any other, cannot be ultimately true except when it speaks about the Only Reality and the falsehood of all else. This is a general standpoint, and there is nothing malicious in the Vedantist position. The Vedantists simply take their stand on the highest realization of the sages. Unfortunately, for those who are not sages and have neither the accompanying love nor the sense of the uniqueness of everything—and such is nearly everyone, by no means excluding the theologians and philosophers—the result is a pitiful haze of vision. Others may not see the woods for the trees near to them; Vedantists are likely not to see the trees for the woods dear to them!

However, we constantly need to return to the sages; they provide the real vitality of any tradition. It is their experiences, actions, and sayings which are systematized by others into scriptures, philosophies, policies, and arguments. Apart from the selflessness (and the accompanying absence of pride) and the natural feelings of compassion and love, which are characteristic of all the sages, there is one feature which needs to be underscored, and which is rarely remarked upon. A sage simultaneously sees the oneness of all there is and the uniqueness of everything. Even if it sounds paradoxical, it is still true in the actual experience of the sages. It is a fact of their existence and behavior that, in relationship with others, the sages are aware that each human being is a manifestation of One Divine Energy, but that at the same time each person presents a unique potential (and the corresponding particular difficulties) and is a wondrously unique expression of the Vastness. Each person is the same—and ultimately all there is is Krishna or *Waheguru* or Brahman—but a person is not replaceable by another as a part in a machine. Each person is a completely unique manifestation of the One. As Nanak says in *Asadi-Var* (The Dawn Hymns), "He himself created creation and gave currency to the Name. And then assumed a second nature and with pleasure regarded his creation seated on his prayer mat."

Uniqueness of the Lion's Roar

To the extent that Hinduism has been influenced by Vedanta, either traditionally or in the modern version of Ramakrishna and Vivekananda, it has a tendency to subsume all religions as different aspects of Hinduism. Furthermore, the closer a person or a doctrine is to the Advaita Vedanta, the closer to Truth is the person or the doctrine assumed to be. In spite of this philosophical proclivity of the Hindu mind, it is not entirely possible to include Christianity and Islam as branches of the great tree of Hinduism. This is so for the obvious reasons of history, language, foreign origins of these religions, and the fact that the Hindus have been for centuries ruled by followers of these religions. But when it comes to the Indians belonging to religions that originated within India, such as Buddhists, Jains, and Sikhs, many Hindus regard them as downright unpatriotic or unspiritual, or both, if they wish to maintain their identity as distinct from the Hindus. Distinctions are just not considered a mark of high enough vision, but are regarded to be the attributes of mere appearances.

Guru Nanak belonged to the great Sant tradition in India, a tradition of Ramananda, Kabir, Dadu, Tukaram, Mira Bai, Chaitanya, and others, expressing itself as the way of love and devotion (bhakti). According to the bhakti tradition, God is the one and only reality; the rest is illusion. God alone needs to be loved, worshiped and adored. Human beings express this love by a complete surrender of their will to the will of God. The language of 'twoness' is as natural and effective in the bhakti tradition, as is that of 'zeroness' (shunyata) in Buddhism (especially in Madhyamika) and 'oneness' in Advaita Vedanta.

Of course, there are other vedantas—Vishishtadvaita Vedanta of

Ramanuja and Dvaita Vedanta of Madhava for example—that are philosophically more hospitable to the path of bhakti. It is, however, a consequence of the profundity and intellectual vigor of Shankara that Vedanta in general is viewed mostly according to his mode. In this mode, the bhakti experience and expression of the twoness is regarded ultimately as inferior to the experience of nonduality, which by its very nature and demand cannot contain or be contained in any forms whatsoever. In the final analysis, as well as experience, either there is a radical negation of all forms, in uttering *neti, neti* (not this, not this), or there is an affirmation—essentially more congenial to the Hindu mind—of existence (sat) not as this or that but as such, consciousness (chit) not of any content but turned upon itself, experience not of anything other but of itself wrapped in its own delight (*ananda*). It is worth noting that Shankara's own personality is in many ways quite paradoxical. In spite of his extreme philosophical position of *keval advaita* (absolute nondualism), he was a great *bhakta* (devotee) and wrote some beautiful and touching hymns. It is possible that the philosophical position he adopted could not do justice to the comprehensiveness of his own experience. He himself seems to have experienced the uniqueness of the other—especially of the Mother Goddess—but by placing it philosophically on a lower level, he did not as much succeed in including it as in creating a duality between jñana and bhakti (witness the later philosophical developments in India).

Among the saints in the Sant tradition, Nanak and Kabir are unique in that they had discernible and strong influences from both the Hindu and the Muslim traditions in India. They had disciples who came to them from both of these religions. At the time of death, in the case of both Kabir and Nanak, their Hindu and Muslim disciples wished to claim their bodies for cremation or burial according to their religious custom. Guru Nanak felt an enormous affinity for Kabir's life and teachings. He saw him as a true saint and lover of God. It is a mark of Kabir's prestige among the gurus and Sikhs in general that seventy-four of his hymns together with 423 shlokas were included in the Adi Granth. Both Kabir and Nanak had a view of God that is quite a subtle and remarkable synthesis of the main thrust of the Abrahamic tradition and the Bharata tradition. Both of them were aware of the situation in which they lived and could hardly ignore the two traditions, and they may have included elements from both in a self-conscious manner.

However, it is important to remark that no truly creative work—in spirituality as much as in science or art—can be self-consciously constructed with elements from here and there. For such a work to have vitality and truth, it must originate from the Source, even though, naturally, it will be expressed in the elements at hand. Thus the teachings of Kabir and Nanak are not construction, put together from the elements of Hinduism and Islam, even though their teachings can be expressed and elaborated in the terms and categories derived from these religions. Nanak and his disciples were neither Hindus nor Muslims; they were unique as Sikhs right from the start, although from a societal point of view the Sikhs may not have acquired a distinct community and church identity until the fifth guru, Guru Arjun. We can get a good idea of the nature of God as understood by Guru Nanak from the opening lines of the morning prayer of the Sikhs, *Japji*:

There is one God.
He is the Supreme truth.
He, the creator,
Is without fear and without hatred.
He, the omnipresent,
Pervades the universe.
He is not born,
Nor does he die to be born again.
By his grace shalt thou worship him.

Before time itself
There was truth.
When time began to run its course
He was the truth.
Even now, he is the truth,
And evermore shall truth prevail.

The readers of the Vedas and the Upanishads would recognize these lines, but so would the readers of the Bible and the Qur'an, even though the latter traditions may differ in their emphasis. For Nanak, God is the Father (*Pita*), Master (*Malik, Sahib*), Husband (*Khasam*), Lover (*Pritam*), but He is also Truth (*sat*), and is formless (*nirankar*). Elsewhere, God is called Rab, Rahim, Ram, Govinda, Hari, Sat Kartar (the true creator), Sat Nam (the true name), or the One whose form is the sacred vibration Aum (Om), Aumkar. For Nanak, God is immanent as well as transcendent, the one reality with which we ultimately merge, but also one whom we worship and obey. With Nanak, even the great Vedic Aumkar became an enunciation of monotheism, as *Ik Aumkar*—there is One God. Ultimately, however, at the deepest level, the innermost core of each person's being is one with God, and when the heart is purified and the mind is still, the light in a person can merge with the Light Eternal.

What is unique with Nanak is the seeming paradox, which is dissolved in his experience, that the Wholly Other is the most intimate kernel of oneself. The emphasis on monotheism here is very Abrahamic, derived from the influence of Islam. The various forms of Vedanta, and in particular Advaita Vedanta, are not and cannot be easy with it. Much of what was taught by Guru Nanak is quite Hindu in flavor, as was also the acceptance by Guru Nanak of the doctrine of karma and reincarnation. It is worth remarking that a fairly similar paradox is presented by the experiences and expressions of Jesus Christ. His remark that "The Father and I are one" (John 10:30) is very congenial to modern Vedantists engaging in ecumenical efforts. This naturally lends itself to an identification with *aham brahmasmi* (I am Brahman) (Brihadaranyaka Upanishad I.4.10). But Christ also said in the same gospel, "The Father is greater than I" (John 14:28). It is this very Father to whose will he surrendered his own, and whom he obeyed even until death. Whatever the philosophical difficulties, and Vedanta always leans to philosophy, Christ himself saw no contradiction in these two statements. Nor would Guru Nanak.

Another area needs to be touched upon briefly. Vedanta, and in particular Advaita Vedanta, by assuming a vantage point which in fact is not in the experience of the vast majority of Vedantists, who cannot be assumed to be the perfect *adhikaris* (possessors) of the *guhyatam rahasyam* (or *rahasyasya rahasyam*, the most esoteric truth), relegates the whole realm of space-time, of particularity, uniqueness, and of history to a lower level, and somehow manages to denigrate it in social practice. Also, from a Vedantist point of view, there cannot be any real point to the distinct manifestations of reality (which is nothing but Brahman) because they are mere variations. In an analogy to be found in the Chandogya Upanishad (VI.1.4), much quoted and admired by the Vedantists, it is said that clay alone is real, while its modifications are only names arising from speech. In the hands of someone without a sensitivity to beauty, this is bound to lead to a facile and destructive dismissal of all art, uniqueness, and individuality. Is an exquisite Chinese vase the same as a lump of clay? Are the statues of the gods at the Somnath temple the same before and after they were smashed? Is it ignorance to resist their destruction? Is there anything in the world for which Guru Gobind Singh might legitimately prepare his chosen warriors, the Khalsa, to fight even until death?

Perhaps this devaluation of history is the greatest point of distinction of Vedanta from the Abrahamic tradition, and also from Sikhism. The world, however little ultimate reality it may have, cannot be ignored. This is what the later Sikh gurus discovered when so many of them and their followers were persecuted by fanatic Muslim rulers. (However, it would be naive to imagine that this persecution would not have taken place if the rulers were orthodox Hindus. The orthodox are never easy with sages who by their very nature are revolutionary, calling into question accepted belief and practice. We can see some likely scenario of a fanatic Hindu reaction to the Sikh gurus in the writings of Dayananda Sarasvati. It is easy to quote scriptures, saying "One is all and all is One," and still beat or even kill an untouchable who might draw water from a brahmin well!) Guru Hargobind, after the execution of Guru Arjun at the orders of Emperor Jahangir, initiated the Sikh community into martial ways. He himself sat at the Akal Takht with two swords as symbolic of spiritual and temporal authority—*Piri* and *Miri*—the combination of bhakti and shakti, of love and power. The great Maratha saint Samartha

Ramdas had met Guru Hargobind and asked him about this change, and he replied, much to the satisfaction of the former: "Internally a hermit, and externally a prince." Arms mean protection of the weak and destruction of the tyrant. Guru Nanak had not renounced the world, he had renounced maya (the sense of attachment and possession). Guru Nanak had spoken of the use of the sword in the real spiritual battle, the battle against oneself. He said, "Overcome the base desires and battle with the mind. Use knowledge as a double-edged sword, then will base desires subside within the mind" (Singh, pp. 315–320). The later gurus were forced by the circumstances prevailing in the world to use not only the inner sword but also the outer sword. They were required to hold onto the Eternal Dharma in the midst of persecution and tyranny. It can be said that the change from the first guru, Guru Nanak, to the tenth guru, Guru Gobind Singh, is somewhat parallel to the change from the Upanishads to the Bhagavad Gita. Krishna's teaching of the Highest Mystery is in the battlefield. There is a continuity, no doubt, but also a different emphasis and form. Whenever dharma is threatened, from the outside or from the inside—as when it becomes merely ritualistic—there is need for engagement in this very world of maya and at this very moment in fleeting time, so that the Mystery which is timeless and at the end of all knowledge (vedanta) could be approached. The outer battle is needed to protect and allow the greater battle inside. Without the Khalsa, vedanta cannot survive. The lions need constantly to guard the temple of the Inner Deity, the Ik Aumkar, the Waheguru. But the lions also need constantly to remember that if they do not dwell in His presence, guarded by Him, their roar would be empty of what truly matters.

The Mill and the Mill-Pond: The Silent Mind of a Yogi

It was the fall of 1965 in New Delhi. My wife had asked me to deliver something to Mrs. Kitty Shivarao, who had been very kind to her when she, four years earlier, had come to India as a volunteer from Canada. I went on my bicycle and came to a sudden stop in front of a very tall man sitting completely alone on a wicker chair on the porch of the Shivarao house. I wondered if Mrs. Shivarao was in, and the man, who was extremely self-contained, said he would go in and look. Without any hurry, but without delay, he got up and went in, and returned to say that she was not in at that time, but I could wait until she came back. I do not recall why I could not wait; perhaps I had the usual haste of the young, especially of those recently returned from a long stay in the West. I handed over to him what I had to deliver to the lady of the house and rode away on my bicycle. But I kept looking back at this unusual man with an extraordinary presence sitting on the porch until I fell off my bicycle, having crashed into a woman carrying a large bundle on her head.

Several months later, at Rajghat in Varanasi, where an interview with J. Krishnamurti had been arranged for me, I was in a great turmoil; I became more and more agitated as four o' clock, the appointed time of the meeting, approached. I was not sure what I needed to ask him. I knew I needed a different kind of knowledge and education than I had obtained in the many schools and universities I had attended. I had become sadder and sadder the closer I had gotten to finishing my Ph.D.: the more I was certified as an educated man by the world, the clearer I was about my ignorance of myself. What little I had gathered about Krishnamurti, mostly from my wife, who had taught for a year in one of his schools in India before we had met, and the little that I had read by him had convinced me that he offered the sort of influence I needed. Here, at last, I was going to meet the great man himself. What was I going to say to him? What did I need to know? What should I ask him? Besides, how could he, or anybody else, say something that would really become a part of myself? After all, I had read what the Buddha had said, and I still behaved the way I did before. And what was I going to tell him about myself? What did I know of any value? What did I have of any value? What was my value? Why waste his time?

All these questions whirled around in my head, making me more and more restless as the time for my meeting with Krishnamurti approached. Then, suddenly, a great calm possessed me. I knew with certainty that I did not know, that nobody else could really tell me something deeply true unless I saw it myself directly, and that there was no escape from an encounter with myself, an encounter without fear and without self-importance. I had no idea what had brought about these realizations and the resulting calm; maybe it was the magic of this extraordinary man working even before I had met him. I walked over to his room with assurance, and precisely at the appointed hour he opened his door. I was surprised to discover that the man in front of me was the same man I had met on the porch in New Delhi. I had difficulty accepting his actual physical size; my first impression of him had no doubt been of his real spiritual height.

He asked me to sit down on the same divan on which he was sitting. Then, after a brief silence, he asked, "What can I do for you?" "Nothing," I said with clarity. "I have really nothing to ask you. I have come just to look at you." He smiled, and we sat in silence for a long time, just looking at each other. Then, no doubt having noticed my attention wandering, he asked what I did and what interested me. I told him, and I also told him about my dissatisfaction with what I had learned. My clarity was dwindling and I was returning to my habitual and more discursive mode of thought. I asked him, "Is there life after death?" He said: "Why worry about death when you don't know anything about life?"

When it was time for me to leave, he took me to the window of his room perched over the river Ganga, overlooking the path which the Buddha had taken on his way to Sarnath after his enlightenment. That was the only time I understood why pilgrims over the centuries have regarded this river as sacred. There were dark, thick clouds over the majestic river, and a white bird was flying in and out of the clouds, sometimes disappearing completely and at other times showing clearly its innocent vulnerability. He put his hand on my shoulder and we stood there watching for a little while; then he said, pointing to the bird in the clouds over the river, "Life is like that: sometimes you see it, sometimes you don't." As I was leaving, he said simply, "We shall meet again."

Many years ago I had written an article called "Letter to J. Krishnamurti" on the invitation of the editors of *A Journal of Our Time*. Rather than getting into an argument with him in the article, for I rarely had any doubt that he was right, I had attempted to say where my own difficulties lay in trying to follow what he had been saying for so many years. This small article had ended with the following: "I am troubled because I do not know how to reconcile the call I hear from your distant shore with the realities where I am. It is clear that a bridge cannot be built from here to There. But can it be built from There to here?" A couple of years after the article had been published, there was an occasion for me to spend some time with Krishnamurti at Ojai in California, the place where he felt most at home. We had a long and intense conversation in the evening, and we were going to meet again at breakfast the next morning. I had asked that he read my little article and respond when we met in the morning. I was eager to know what he would say. He said he liked the last sentence, and added: "A bridge can be built from There to here." He would not say much more about it, except to imply that that is what he had been talking about all these years.

Since I have been interested for a long time in the quality of attention and seeing which can bring about an action in oneself so that a radical change can take place naturally, from the inside, I asked Krishnamurti about it. For him thought leads to fragmentation, and subsequently to fear and sorrow, as for the Buddha *tanha* (selfish craving) leads to dukkha (sorrow) or for the Vedantist *avidya* (ignorance) leads to maya (illusion). In all of these teachings, what is required for sorrow, fear, and illusion to be dissolved in the clear light of intelligence and truth is total attention. I asked him about the nature of this attention, and said, "What I find in myself is the fluctuation of attention." He said with emphasis, "What fluctuates is not attention. Only inattention fluctuates."

On another occasion he said to me, "I am still very shy, but I used to be much worse. I would stand behind the platform from where I was supposed to speak to an audience, and shake. One day I saw the total absurdity of it, and the shaking left me. I was free of it for ever."

In a conversation in Madras he said that the intelligence beyond thought is just there, like the air, and does not need to be created by discipline or effort. "All one needs to do is to open the window." I suggested that most windows are painted shut and need a lot of scraping before they can be opened, and asked, "How does one scrape?" "Sir," he said sadly, "You don't see that the house is on fire."

In his concern with the dangers of hierarchy, Krishnamurti frequently placed a great deal of emphasis on being democratic. He would often talk in a small group as if everyone were actually at the same level as himself and had an equal right to express his opinion. Soon, of course, he would get bored or impatient with a mere exchange of opinions, and speak with the force of clear seeing, commanding attention from everyone around him. On one of these occasions in India, he had given a long rope to many people's opinions about the nature of the religious mind. I had just flown in from North America, and was not eager to spend the morning philosophizing or listening to various opinions. He was the one I wanted to hear, for I had understood some time ago that Krishnamurti had a completely unusual mind and that he saw many things with an extraordinary clarity not vouchsafed to many. On this occasion, anxious to hear him speak, I blurted out, "But, Krishna Ji, what do you have to say about it? After all, you are the cat with the meat." I realized immediately that I had not chosen a very felicitous American expression for the assembled company of vegetarians. After a brief pause, he smiled, relieving the tension created by my remark, and protested that he was not special. "Do you think K is a freak?" he said, referring to himself in the third person, using only the initial of his name, assuming it to be obvious that he wasn't. I was never convinced nor was anyone else around him, as far as I could see.

So often I had been completely frustrated by going around the same point with Krishnamurti; for example, his insistence that there can be a radical transformation instantaneously, without any discipline or path or guidance, and by my inability to even understand what he was saying, let alone do it. On one occasion, in a semi-public seminar, I said in despair, "There's no sense in carrying on. We keep going around the same mulberry bush. It's totally frustrating." "Sir, then why do you keep coming?" I knew that my coming had nothing to do with any reasons, so I said what was true, "Because I love you." One did not decide to love Krishnamurti any more than a flower decides to give fragrance, to use one of his favorite analogies.

Once when I was in London I learned that Krishnamurti was at Brockwood, not very far away. Naturally, I wanted to see him. Not succeeding in making a telephone connection with anybody there, I gave up after many attempts. Since on many occasions he had said, "You may come any time," I decided to drive over with a friend and take my chances. I wonder if the gods know how heavily guarded the gates of paradise have to be! One could say that there were lots of guardians at his gates, and we had some difficulty, quite understandable to be sure, in getting close to the inner sanctum. One burly woman, in some sort of command at the place, was especially offended at our audacity in thinking that we could see Krishnamurti himself without a prior appointment. She was a proper lion! I thought she actually had a point, although I wondered how Krishnamurti would have responded to her description of him when she growled at us, "Anybody can walk in off the street and want to see the high and the mighty!"

I knew we were not supposed to be there, and I had not really expected to see Krishnamurti, but I was like an iron filing naturally drawn by this magnet. I had not analyzed the situation and decided on a course of action; it just had not occurred to me that I could be within driving distance and not go to meet him. While leaving, for some reason I reached into my pocket and found a visiting card, which I gave to the lion to deliver to Mary Zimbalist, who for the last many years had selflessly devoted herself to taking care of Krishnamurti, often traveling with him. She took the card from me with much hesitation, and I was not sure she was going to deliver it, but we tarried a little anyway. Soon I saw Mary hurrying toward us with a big smile. She greeted me and my friend most affectionately, explaining that things had been very hectic all morning: the BBC was filming a program on Krishnamurti and a senior man from the *Times* of London was doing an interview. In any case, of course we must stay for lunch, and Krishna Ji will be along any minute now. Soon he appeared and welcomed us very warmly. At lunch, he looked fatigued and did not eat much. We spoke about this and that, and I wondered to myself how can this man at such an advanced age travel so much. What does he hope to accomplish? Can it be accomplished by talking to large numbers of people? Isn't some sort of preparation required to make use of what he is saying? He said, "You should have been here in the morning; we had a wonderful discussion; a lot came out." I asked, "Can any real transformation take place just with discussion?" "No, sir," he said.

Krishnamurti's destiny was obviously to be a teacher, even though he tried strenuously to avoid being so labeled. He especially eschewed the devotional sort of adulation he received everywhere, particularly in India. After a public lecture in Madras we went for a walk together. I wondered why he was trying to sneak out of the compound by a side door like a thief rather than walk out the main gate. "No, sir, they'll start touching my feet and all. Oh, God, no!" He had a special feeling for solitude. Even when walking with others he often preferred silence. We walked for a while in complete silence along the beach in Adyar. Suddenly he seemed to remember that I was in town with my children, who went swimming there. "Mefiez vous; faites attention!" He knew I dabbled a bit in French; he particularly liked that and would occasionally say a few sentences to me in that language. He was warning me to make sure that my children realized that there was a strong undertow at that place and that they took proper precautions. I thanked him and wondered if he swam there himself. "I know this place well. You know this is where K was discovered by them!" he said conspiratorially.

I was supposed to meet him one evening in Ojai. When I arrived I found him working in the orange orchard pruning some trees. We stayed there a little while. He told me casually, "The speaker used to have healing powers, clairvoyance, and all that. They have told me this; I don't know." He showed me the tree under which the "process" took place. He spoke very tenderly of his younger brother, with whom he had lived in the cottage nearby. We stood there for a few minutes. He seemed to be actually seeing his brother there, and I think (I am not completely sure of this) he said that was the place where his brother had died. After a little while, I asked him, "What exactly is the 'process'?" I knew immediately that I had chosen a wrong moment to ask this. He looked at me sadly and said, "This is what everyone wants to know. Then they will start imitating it and faking it. No, it cannot be said."

I had often been struck by a similarity between the all-or-nothing absolutist stance of Krishnamurti and that of many Old Testament prophets. I was also sure that essentially, more than anything else, he was a lover at heart: a lover of nature, of presence, of truth, and of silence. I was delighted and not at all surprised when he told me, in response to a question of mine, that his favourite book in the Bible was The Song of Songs. I told him that the great Rabbi Aqiba had declared that book to be the holiest of the holies, and that he had said that all the ages were not worth the day when this book was given to Israel. Krishnamurti was only mildly interested in Rabbi Aqiba's comment about it, but was delighted when I recalled a line: "I sleep, but my heart waketh: it is the voice of my beloved that knocketh."

I had been asked by the editors of an encyclopedia to write an article on Krishnamurti. I prepared the outline and made extensive notes, and had a special interview with him to make sure that what I had written accurately reflected his thought. I asked him whether "intelligence beyond thought" was the central thing that he spoke about. He agreed, but without much feeling. Suddenly, he was animated: "Take the risk, sir. Say what you wish. If you speak from the heart, I'll agree. Take the risk."

Once I was visiting Ojai, having promised Mary Zimbalist before coming there that I would not engage Krishna Ji in serious talk, since he was taking a few days rest after a strenuous lecture series. In any case, I did not have anything specific to ask him; I simply wanted to be in his presence. I was in the kitchen talking to the cook when Krishnamurti entered by the side door on his way to lunch. He saw me and extended his hand with a broad smile. I took his hand and then hugged him. When he inquired after my wife and children, I gave him another hug from them. He was a little surprised, perhaps not being used to receiving physical affection. There were about a dozen people at lunch, talking about this and that. As lunch was ending, I said something about the subtle alchemical changes left in the body by an insight. Unexpectedly, he reached across the table, held my hand and said, "Sir, shall we go into it seriously?" "Some other time, Krishna Ji. Now it is time for you to have a rest," I said. He looked quite annoyed, as if we had no sense of the right priority of things. He insisted that we talk seriously there and then, and asked for a tape recorder to be brought to record it. I looked at Mary to convey, "Look, it's not my fault. He is the one getting himself into it." She tried to suggest that we could talk later in the afternoon, but he would not hear any of it.

So we had a serious conversation for a long time. At one point I said, "A new insight belongs to a new body, it seems to me. What do you think of that, Krishna Ji?" "You know, sir, it occurs to me that K does not *think* at all. That's strange. He just *looks*."

Once when I told him that he was a real scientist, a scientist of the interior, he seemed to like that. After a long silence, he said, "I have been going around the world talking for more than sixty years. Nobody understands what I am trying to say, especially the scientists. They are too clever for their own good." "You know, Krishna Ji, if they understood what you are saying, they wouldn't let you into the country. You are completely subversive." He laughed, "That's right, sir, don't tell them."

The last time I was in Ojai, it was as a guest of the Krotona Institute, where I had been invited to give a few lectures. Naturally, I went to see Krishnamurti as often as I could. He seemed to take a particularly mischievous delight in the fact that the Theosophists were paying for me to come and see him. "Keep it up, sir. Don't tell them. Sneak out and come here as often as you can."

Since I had been so fascinated by the special nature and quality of Krishnamurti's mind, I often returned to that subject with him and he would frequently speak about the religious mind and its innocence, freshness, and vulnerability. I was more interested in the particularities of his mind. The more he tried to convince me to the contrary, the more I seemed to feel that Krishnamurti was in fact a freak. "What is the nature of your own mind, Krishna Ji? What do you see when you look at that tree?" "My mind is like a mill-pond. Any disturbance that is created in it soon dies, leaving it unruffled as before," he said calmly. Then, as if reading what I was about to ask, he added with the most playful smile, "And your mind is like a mill!"

The last time I met him was in May 1985, in Ojai, just before his ninetieth birthday. We had a long talk about death. During the conversation I had raised the same question which I had asked twenty years earlier. At the end he said, "The real question is 'Can I die while I am living? Can I die to all my collections—material, psychological, religious?' If you can die to all that, then you'll find out what is there after death. Either there is nothing; absolutely nothing. Or there *is* something. But you cannot find out until you actually die while living. Don't accept it. No believing is necessary. Doubt it; question it."

When I was leaving he came to the door and held it open. He looked a little frail, and I did not want him to stand there waiting while I put on my socks and shoes, which I had taken off at the entrance. My heart had been filled by what he had said, and I was taking my leave slowly. When I said again that he should go in and not wait there, he said, "The noble never close the door."

Gurdjieff Work and the Teaching of Krishna

"If I were to cease working," says Krishna in the Bhagavad Gita (3.24), "all these worlds would perish." He advises his friend and disciple, Arjuna, to act on his own level and scale as Krishna himself acts on the highest level and on the largest scale. So are seekers firmly and repeatedly advised in the Gurdjieff Work to work on their own level, that of the earth, lest the earth should collapse.

This is not the place to discuss the question of any historical links between the teaching of Gurdjieff and India. Gurdjieff was widely traveled and may have been influenced by various strands of the vast Indian tradition—either directly or indirectly through Tibet and other parts of Asia. He refers to India on many occasions in his writings, often with the suggestion that in ancient times, if not now, esoteric schools with real knowledge had existed there. He even referred to himself as a 'Hindu' in his first public announcement in a Moscow newspaper in 1914 regarding the performance of an Indian mystery play called *The Struggle of the Magicians*. This particular instance may not be anything more than a useful role playing, but there is no doubt that he was very knowledgeable about Indian traditions and often mercilessly critical of their exaggerations and of the many fads derived from India which were current in the occult and spiritualist circles of his day.

One cannot fail to be struck by the many parallels between the Gurdjieff Work and the teaching of Krishna, as well as other traditional teachings. However, every teaching has its own specificity, a particular center of gravity and area of emphasis. The important thing is to remark that no real teaching can be made by the ordinary human mind, here below. There cannot be a way from here to There, unless the way is laid down from There to here. No teaching can be true unless it originates from above, by the Will of Heaven. Great teachers and messengers from above are needed in order to assist in the descent of heavenly wisdom by preparing the right ground of being—body, mind, and heart. Gurdjieff's teaching is not *personal* any more than are the teachings of the Buddha or of the Christ. He lays no claim to any subjective or private invention of his ideas; on the contrary, he continually stresses the antiquity of his ideas and practices. They are *original* only in the sense that they originate from the Source and carry the potential of relating sincere practitioners to the origins. However, the Work is unique and fresh. And it is demanding, for it requires a total response. Gurdjieff's pupils recall him saying about his teaching, "This, no cheap thing!" Madame Jeanne de Salzmann, who inherited the mantle of responsibility for the Work after Gurdjieff's death in 1949, often quoted Gurdjieff's remark that "Very good is not enough."

It is to be expected that genuine teachings would naturally have much in common at depth. They are likely to be different from each other at the surface, owing to different emphases arising in response to contingencies of time, place and language. Every teaching belongs to its time, utilizing the specific modality of thought and idiom relevant to the people who are addressed by the teaching, but every teaching invites those who hear it to respond to what is true with an objective vibration quite independent of their own subjectivity. Completely lawfully, as is explained in detail by Gurdjieff using the Law of Seven, as reported by Ouspensky in *In Search of the Miraculous* and a is indicated by Krishna (BG 4.1–3), every teaching is subject to the ravages of time. Unless great care is taken in maintaining the original vibration—which must not be confused with the old forms—or unless there is a continual revitalization, continuous degeneration is inevitable.

Most of us, whether from the East or the West, have been cut off from the living waters of the great traditions, which are constantly menaced by the twin forces of sentimentality and scholasticism. Great texts exist, as do wonderful ceremonies and rituals rich with meaning and knowledge, but they do not have an action on the whole of our being. Our eyes are dulled and we do not see clearly; we do not dwell in our right mind from which we might comprehend their meaning. Cleansing of our eyes and connecting us with our right mind is the purpose of the teaching and the practice of the Work. It is quite reasonable to ask what light the traditions shed on the Gurdjieff teaching. But, in fact, seekers engaged on this path often realize, through their deep personal experience, that the traditions get charged with meaning for them by their contact with the teaching of Gurdjieff. It brings fresh insight to the old formulations and a practical way of relating with the depth of ourselves as well as with the depth of the traditions.

It is true that, rightly understood, the tradition is always right; but it is also true that the tradition is almost always misunderstood, especially when taken externally and partially, with exaggerated emphasis on rational speculation or on sentimental devotion. We can see this historically: if the traditions had not been misunderstood there would not have been such a forceful challenge thrown at the official guardians of the traditions by Krishna or the Buddha or the Christ. One sees not only that the traditions are continually betrayed but also that the traditions themselves betray the truth—as is implied by one of the root meanings of the word 'tradition'. Whenever a scholastic interpretation freezes the tradition in a rigid formulation, however liberating it had once been and however hallowed by time, one needs especially to recall the words of Krishna that "For a brahmin [seeker of Brahman, the Vastness] who truly knows, there is as much use in all the Vedas [sacred texts] as there is in a well when there is a flood of water on all sides" (BG 2:46).

In our days, Gurdjieff brought a revitalizing challenge to the traditions, not in order to destroy them but in order to recover and release their essential core from the encrustation of dogma, exclusivism, and mechanical repetition. Gurdjieff was a traditionalist—although from all accounts a very untraditional one—in the sense that he had an enormous respect for the traditions and believed that all the major traditions once carried a kernel of truth which has in general been lost and which may be recovered from the fragments that have been preserved in the sacred texts and ceremonies of many religions. He referred to his teaching as 'esoteric Christianity'; but one feels that in other contexts he might equally have called it 'esoteric Buddhism' or 'esoteric Islam'. 'Esoteric' does not refer to any concealment, but rather to a level that is subtler and more inner, and that is not available to the ordinary, unintegrated mind and heart. In order to approach the esoteric level a preparation is needed: a preparation not only to understand truth but also to withstand it. More than anything else, this requires a sacrifice of our mental and emotional habits that keep us tethered to our present mechanical level.

One particularly striking example of a habit of thought in connection with the Indian tradition is that of *kundalini,* which is said to be a force that is situated, coiled up like an earring or a serpent, at the base of the spine, in the *chakra* (subtle center of energy in the body) representing the earth (*prithivi*). In most religious and philosophic circles in India, especially those fascinated by occult phenomena, kundalini is given a very high valuation. But Gurdjieff has nothing positive to say about kundalini. Having undertaken, as he himself says in the preface to his book *All and Everything: Beelzebub's Tales to His Grandson*, "to destroy mercilessly, without any compromises whatsoever, in the mentation and feelings of the reader, the beliefs and views, by centuries rooted in him, about everything existing in the world," he ascribes to the suggestively parallel organ *kundabuffer* the property of making human beings perceive reality topsy-turvy. Ouspensky quotes Gurdjieff as saying, "In reality Kundalini is the power of imagination, the power of fantasy, *which takes the place of a real function.* ... Kundalini can act in all centers and with its help all the centers can be satisfied with the imaginary instead of the real. ... Kundalini is a force put into men in order to keep them in their present state. If men could really see their true position and could understand all the horror of it, they would be unable to remain where they are even for one second. They would begin to seek a way out and they would quickly find it, *because there is a way out*; but men fail to see simply because they are hypnotized. Kundalini is the force that keeps them in a hypnotic state. 'To awaken' for man means to be 'dehypnotized'" (Ouspensky, *In Search of the Miraculous*, p. 220).

As we recover from the shock dealt by Gurdjieff's merciless criticism of one of the precious jewels of Indian spirituality, we can begin to look at the tradition again. We discover that the most thorough and insightful authority on yoga, Patañjali, the author of the celebrated *Yoga Sutra*, never mentions kundalini, and some of the very ancient and authoritative texts on yoga, such as *Yoga Yajñavalkya*, regard kundalini to be a hindrance in the spiritual evolution of a person, an impediment that needs to be removed in order to be touched and transformed by the energy from heaven. The human being is situated along an axis stretched from heaven to earth, and the proper inner order demands a flow of energy (prana) from above downward. Naturally, the powers from below, entrenched and coiled up in the organism as kundalini, resist and try to block the entry and movement of prana from above. It may be useful to quote a contemporary authority on yoga in this regard: "If you analyze what I have been saying, you will see that *kundalini* is nothing but what has been called *avidya* [ignorance]. In the same way that *avidya* has become so powerful that it stops *purusha* [spirit, the very person] from seeing, *kundalini* blocks *prana* from entering the *sushumna* [the central channel in the body for the flow of *prana*]" (T. K. V. Desikachar, *The Heart of Yoga*, p. 244).

Although I was born and brought up in India and although I learned the Bhagavad Gita by heart as a boy, this ancient text remained inaccessible. It is only after I encountered the ideas and practices of the Work that the text became really sacred for me: more profound, more universal, and much more existentially engaging than before.

Both Gurdjieff and Madame de Salzmann constantly emphasize the importance of struggling against one's habitual nature, the automaton that I call myself. This self, including the psyche and the body, is the battleground in which the forces of the real I, the Self (Atman), and those of mechanicality, inattention, and unconsciousness fight. The symbolic setting of the Bhagavad Gita is quite rightly a battleground. Krishna says in the Mahabharata that human beings do not have a choice between war and peace; the only choice is about the level of the warrior's struggle. There are subtler and subtler levels on which the battle has to be fought again and again: inside oneself, there are forces of opposition, resistance, and discord as much as there are forces of aspiration seeking right order. Arjuna, and by extension each one of us, has only this choice: we can be compelled by our own nature, which is Nature (Prakriti) following her laws in miniature, to struggle and suffer as a victim of the cosmic drama, or we can see the necessity to labor and to suffer intentionally as an instrument of Krishna's purposes. In undertaking the struggle as yajña (sacrifice as a way of exchange with higher levels), Arjuna assists in the maintenance and upholding of proper order (dharma).

Gurdjieff realized that contemporary human beings cannot respond to the traditional religious ways based on faith, hope, or love. He quotes the deliberations of the Very Saintly Ashiata Shiemash, a messenger from Above, concerning the terror of the human situation:

> *During the period of my year of special observations on all of their [human beings'] manifestations and perceptions, I made it categorically clear to myself that although the factors for engendering in their presences the sacred being-impulses of Faith, Hope, and Love are already quite degenerated in the beings of this planet [Earth], nevertheless, the factor which ought to engender that being-impulse on which the whole psyche of beings of a three-brained system is in general based, and which impulse exists under the name of Objective-Conscience, is not yet atrophied in them, but remains in their presences almost in its primordial state.*
>
> *Thanks to the abnormally established conditions of external ordinary being-existence existing here, this factor has gradually penetrated and become embedded in that consciousness which is here called "subconsciousness," in consequence of which it takes no part whatever in the functioning of their ordinary consciousness (Gurdjieff, p. 359).*

Gurdjieff taught ways of awakening *objective conscience*—which has as much to do with a feeling perception of higher reality as with a direct insight into oneself, almost always producing remorse of conscience, yet without loss of hope. The teaching of Gurdjieff involves the body, feeling, and intellect, and not solely one or another. Even though different components of the Work may at different times demand more from one or another aspect of the total human being, the overall emphasis is on the harmonization of all the parts. The Work is also called the Fourth Way, as distinct from the ways that somewhat exclusively emphasize physical discipline and asceticism, or faith and devotion, or reasoning and knowledge. All these other aspects are not ignored in the Work, but are rather integrated in a comprehensive whole. It can be said that the fourth way is for "man number four" who does not have a lopsided development of the mind or the emotions or the body, and in whom the various psychic centers are in some balance. A proper balance and equilibrium of the centers can be said to be an intermediate aim of the Work, so that what is above the centers can have the possibility of embodiment for a conscious action in the world.

With this background of the Work, one questions the traditional interpretations of the Bhagavad Gita, which enumerate the various yogas (ways, disciplines, practices) and almost always emphasize one or the other. The different yogas that usually get mentioned are: karma yoga of action, bhakti yoga of love, jñana yoga of gnosis, and dhyana yoga of meditation. A closer examination of the text, always keeping an eye on the actual practice and not adhering exclusively to a theoretical study, reveals that the overall yoga enunciated by Krishna for the transformation of Arjuna is that of buddhi yoga. As was discussed earlier, the various other yogas constitute limbs of buddhi yoga, as do the diverse musical instruments in an orchestra, and are called and emphasized at different times in the symphony. This yoga is based on the awakening of buddhi, the integrated intelligence and will. 'Buddhi' is derived from the same root from which 'buddha' is derived; the verbal root is 'budh', meaning to wake up, to discern. Buddhi is the faculty of higher vision, of discernment, of attention, and it is above the ordinary mind (manas) and the senses. Buddhi seems to be a composite of the higher emotional and the higher intellectual centers in Gurdjieff's teaching, as manas is a composite of the lower mind and emotions.

In an unintegrated person, the desire-will—which arises mostly from the senses, from likes-dislikes, pleasures and fears—runs the mind. Such a mind, in its turn, dissipates the vision of buddhi into conflicting desires. If a person is integrated, there is a reversal of this uneducated natural order and the establishment of the right order. The proper internal order is a prerequisite for the maintenance of external order. External dharma is possible only after the right internal order is established, which is possible only through spiritual discipline (yoga). Yoga is any discipline or way or path for the transformation of a human being, from a state of fragmentation to a state of integration, from the monkey-mind to the Buddha mind.

There is a persistent tendency in the spiritual traditions of India, more pronounced in the schools influenced by Vedanta, to regard the whole of the manifested creation—of individuality, time, space, energy and substance—as an unholy mistake that needs to be undone by a spiritual person. It is worth remarking that the Bhagavad Gita itself is unique in the Indian tradition in its emphasis on action here and now, on the body as a vehicle of yajña and dharma. Krishna's teaching, just as that of Gurdjieff, is not to make us angels but to make us truly human—whole, complete, and integrated.

The Indian spiritual traditions have been so occupied with the *oneness* of all there is, that the *uniqueness* of a person, with specific responsibility and possibility, tends to be ignored. In this view there is only one reality, and that is Brahman; everything else is false. Plurality may be allowed, but only at a lower level of relative truth, of ignorance. Distinctions are just not considered a mark of a high enough vision, and are mere appearances. This point of view, although seemingly derived from the highest realization of the sages, is only theoretical and not connected with the actual experience of the sages. It relegates the whole realm of space-time, of particularity, uniqueness, and of history to a lower level, and somehow manages to denigrate it.

A sage simultaneously sees the oneness of all there is and the uniqueness of everything. It is a fact of their existence and behavior that, in relationship with others, the sages are aware that each human being is a manifestation of one divine energy, but that at the same time each person presents a unique potential and a wondrously unique expression of the Vastness. Each person is related with the oneness, but a person is not replaceable by another as a part in a machine. Ultimately all there is is Krishna or Brahman, or, as Madame de Salzmann said, everything comes from the same conscious energy, but the One is expressed uniquely in each manifestation. With a thorough self-knowledge, a person becomes a sage, a *mahapurusha* (great person), who, as a microcosmos, is able to mirror all the aspects of the great cosmos. Such a sage becomes a *first person universal*, who sees each of us as both one with the Source and uniquely ourselves.

We can easily get the impression from much of Indian spirituality that *individuality* is an illusion which a sage sheds when enlightened. Given the emphasis placed by Gurdjieff on the development of true individuality, we need to look again. Acquiring true individuality or 'an indivisible I' means that human beings have "in their presences every possibility for becoming particles of a part of Divinity" (Gurdjieff, p. 452). It is true that Krishna teaches the renunciation of the egotistic self (*samkalpa atma*), but he does not advise the abandonment of individuality (svabhava), which is the true representative in each person of Krishna himself, the Very Atma, the Real Self. According to Krishna, the integration of a person is possible only through the discovery of svabhava, the essential being. One of the basic teachings in the Bhagavad Gita is that we cannot really be free without following our own svabhava, manifested in the corresponding svadharma and svakarma. That is to say, only those undertakings and actions which correspond to our innermost tendencies and our proper place in the cosmic scheme can lead to freedom.

Of course, this freedom is only from a particular level of existence, and it is possible only when the demands of that level are fulfilled. Otherwise, as Krishna says, each of us is compelled to return again and again to our own deepest unsatisfied yearnings. Human incarnation is necessary, useful, and sacred; it takes place for the purpose of undertaking action, which is required for the maintenance of inner and outer order. The world is real, even though in general we live in a fantasy world of our own making and not in the real world.

It is necessary to make one more remark in connection with the understanding of individuality. In Indian thought, and in particular in the *Yoga Sutra*, the first manifestation of fundamental ignorance (avidya) is said to be asmita, which is often translated as 'individuality'. Literally what it means is 'I am this' or 'I am that'. This expression is deceptively close to I AM, which refers to a practice significant in the gospels and sacred in the Work. A good illustration is found in the title of the third series of Gurdjieff's writings, *Life Is Real Only Then, When 'I Am'*. I AM is the practice of awareness and participation in the fullness of Being, and always leads to humility, whereas asmita is a limitation of Being by specification and restriction, and therefore leads to smallness and self-importance.

Madame de Salzmann often emphasized the need to watch for the subtle point of transition between making an effort, which is done by the ego, and the letting go of the ego-effort so that what is higher, and therefore unknown to the ego, and certainly not in its control, may enter and transform the self from above. Real and true action is from above and cannot be controlled from below. In the terminology of the Bhagavad Gita, a person can woo Krishna, not compel him. That is why a proper aspirant is simultaneously an active warrior and a lover—until becoming a receptive beloved, knowing when to assert and when to surrender: beloved above and warrior below.

Having admonished Arjuna to carry out his proper dharma and to act like the good warrior that he is, Krishna says toward the end of the Bhagavad Gita, "Relinquishing all dharmas, take refuge in Me alone; I shall deliver you from all evil; be not grieved" (18:66). A person may abandon all dharmas and efforts if completely disciplined and vigilant against distractions from below. Rightly aligned and ordered, one is a spacious vessel filled from above. Such a person is a miniature Krishna, a microcosmic human, assisting the maintenance of the cosmos by alchemical Work.

But what is true at the mountaintop is not true at the base. This teaching is "most secret (esoteric) of all secrets" (BG 18:63), and as Krishna warns "is not to be spoken by you to anyone who is without austerity, not dedicated and not obedient" (BG 18:67). We must not abandon right action, effort, and dharma out of cowardice, self-pity, or laziness. Only a warrior earns the right to be a lover, and then to be the beloved. Ultimately, of course, it is less important to know Krishna or to love him than to be known and loved by him.

It is almost inevitable that in any tradition the words accompanying the sightings from the mountaintop will sooner or later be reproduced in the textbooks of philosophy and religion, and these will be read, argued about, and debated, without the accompanying practice which alone could assist in the embodiment of vision. It is in order to guard against this partialization and degeneration of vision that it is highly recommended traditionally that a seeker should work with a master who embodies the teaching, and remains in a dynamic exchange with the levels above and the levels below. A practical teacher always has a necessary reminder, as in the following pertinent remark of Madame de Salzmann: "The religious people talk about the Lord, the *Seigneur*. That is an energy of a very high level. They say the Lord helps me; that is true, but something is required of me. I have to prepare myself for this Seigneur to help" (*Heart Without Measure*, p. 74).

Sentimentality and scholasticism are the two main avenues by which the vitality of any spiritual tradition is drained. This has also happened in India. Merely mental understanding of the peak vision of the sages in which Atman is said to be one with Brahman, that is, the deepest self of a person is the same as the highest Absolute, has tended to make us forget the actual situation in which we are very far from the realization of this supreme identity. Unless we recognize our actual situation, and suffer the fact of our alienation from the Real, nothing can in fact change. In the crucible of that suffering, that which keeps us attached to the surface levels of ourselves may be dissolved. "Stay in front of your inadequacy," repeatedly exhorted Madame de Salzmann; "suffer the fact that you are in pieces!" (*Heart Without Measure*, p. 65).

The significant aspect of any true teaching, whether of Krishna or of Gurdjieff, is the preparation of the entire human being to be able to receive the energy and substance from above. Quite typically in the Indian philosophical tradition, the highest resides in the deepest part of the person. The person is not limited by the physical body, nor is the boundary between the inner and the outer determined by the skin. There are subtler and subtler levels within a person and one can come to a realer self if one is willing and able to pay the requisite price—namely, that of the sacrifice of the samkalpa atma (fantasy self). One of the strongest memories I have of Madame de Salzmann is her sitting like a combination of a tiger and a hawk, compassionate in the hope she emanated and terrifying in the objective demand, asking "Are you willing to pay the price?"

Work, like yajña in the Bhagavad Gita, is the occasion, or the process or the means for an exchange of substances or energies between levels of being. An invocation of higher forces (devas, gods) or a feeding of them is yajña. The gods sustain human beings through yajña, and are in their turn nourished by human beings through yajña, in a cycle of reciprocal maintenance (BG 3:10–13). The whole universe is created as yajña and is sustained through it. We cannot live without participation in the cosmic rite, the universal yajña, and we are either instruments or victims. Through the voluntary act of sacrifice, in particular the purusha yajña, a person offers the self in sacrifice. In this, the self is the sacrificer, the ego-self is the oblation, and the Real Self is the eater of sacrifice. In becoming food for the Self, the ego becomes sacred; in sacrificing one's self-will, a person can be willed by the Self.

Without a true internal integration, we are fragmented and in pieces; there is discord inside, adding to the discord outside. What is necessary, as Gurdjieff said, is to die to our ordinary self while still alive, that is to our habits and attachments. Only when the requisite price has been paid can a new birth take place. Work is needed in order to make contact with higher levels—a living, substantial contact, not only in rational philosophy or in wishful poetry. It is appropriate to quote a fragment of a letter that Madame de Salzmann wrote: "It is a moment when the ideas are not enough. There is a force, a higher one; it is in us, but can have no action as long as our state does not allow it—as long as our centres are not related. At that stage the ideas do not cooperate, one has to feel the inner inadequacy, be touched, suffer from it and give all one's attention to this inner relation which will open the door to the higher energy" (*Heart Without Measure*, p. 115).

Yoga off the Mat

Yoga in Daily Life

Renouncing all actions on Me,
Mindful of your inner self,
Without expectation and selfishness,
Fight, without agitation. (BG 3:30)

Here Krishna invites us and enjoins us to make our daily life into a spiritual practice, a yoga. No one can be without action. Even if we simply lie down, doing nothing visible, we are still engaged in action. "Because no one can remain actionless even for a moment. Everyone is driven to action, helplessly indeed, by the forces of nature" (BG 3.05). Even if the body is still, the mind is in action, associating this with that, dreaming, desiring something, fearing something else. The question is not whether to act but how to act. Similarly, no one can avoid daily life; the question is not whether we should participate in daily life, but rather how to participate in this life we live daily.

What Is Daily Life?

All the actions we do routinely—sleeping, eating, washing, walking, sitting, standing, talking—are included in our daily life. And so are all the activities we engage in as a part of our jobs, professions, household routines and the like. These are not without their importance, but our inquiry here has less to do with the various kinds of activities and much more to do with the quality of the actor engaged in these activities—willingly or unwillingly, driven by nature or driven by the spirit—because our daily activities reflect the quality of our being. When Krishna speaks to Arjuna about a person of steady wisdom (*sthitaprajña*) (BG 56), Arjuna does not ask what sort of wonderful ideas such a person has or what the theology or philosophy a person of steady wisdom is. He asks: "How does a person of steady wisdom, who is established in samadhi, speak? How does he sit? How does he walk?" (BG 2:54).

Krishna's answer is quite unambiguous: "A person of steady wisdom is one who has become free of all desires that prey upon the mind, and who is content and at peace. When unpleasant things do not disturb, nor pleasures beguile, when craving, fear, and anger have left, such a one is a sage of steady wisdom" (BG 2:55–56).

There is a Hasidic story, which is also echoed in Zen circles, that tells of a pupil who goes to the master not as much to hear a learned discourse than to see how the master ties his shoe laces, to see how the master lives. And in our daily life we walk, talk, sit, and tie our shoe laces. We express our understanding and we search for steady wisdom in the midst of these very activities.

When we hope to move away from daily life, what do we expect to escape from? Do we hope to escape from the ordinariness, the repeatability, and the predictability of our daily life? Do we wish for adventure, for something unexpected, for something that will surprise us—perhaps an unexpected gift or a guest or an event? There is much to be said for new impressions that can bring our mechanical routine into question. There is value in going to new places, meeting new people and new ideas. We are refreshed by the unexpected; something other than the usual comes alive in us, and we feel reinvigorated and rejuvenated. But many things are still the same. Even on the final ascent to Mount Everest there are elements of daily life. Certainly in the monastery—which for some might seem like a release from daily life into a realm of spirituality—the activities of daily life are required. Many requirements, mostly to do with the general maintenance of our bodies and of our places of shelter, are the same or very similar everywhere.

I once met a monk in a Buddhist monastery in Thailand. He had the venerable traditional name of Nagasena. At that time, he had been a monk for nearly thirty years, as long as I had been a professor. We were instantly drawn to each other, and spent practically the whole night speaking together. He said to me, "You know, being a monk is a profession like any other. It has its ups and downs, its routine, its excitement, and its dullness. It is just like daily life."

When we think of daily life as a dull affair, consisting of ordinary activities, we are referring to a level of the mind, to a level of awareness and of engagement, which is dull and humdrum. When we wish to be released from daily life, it is this level of life and engagement that we wish to escape. We wish to live with another level of engagement—one in which we are not bored, or dispersed; in which we are more alive to ourselves and to everything around us. Those who are freshly in love have no complaints about daily life. It is the lack of a love affair with life that makes everything stale and dull and uninteresting. We can be connected with the same quality of engagement while washing dishes in a kitchen or praying in a monastery on Mount Athos.

Another aspect of life that mitigates against our sense of freedom is that of reward and punishment. What we call daily life—especially as contrasted with a holiday, or with retired life—is the feeling of being constrained by reward and punishment, by the hope of gain or the fear of loss. So we dream of another life—perhaps in a monastery or perhaps at a resort—where we will not be driven by gain or loss, or reward and punishment, or ambition and fear, at least not in the ordinary sense of gain or loss. In this dream, we seek a satisfaction of some subtler kind, a reward of heaven perhaps, or a gain for our soul, but nothing crass or materialistic. The subtler part of ourselves feels overwhelmed by the excessive demands of worldly life or is disenchanted by the crudity of this life.

However, what we wish to escape from in our ordinary life resides not as much in what we actually do as in the quality of engagement with it and the motivations underlying the activities. The dullness or ordinariness of daily life is not as much characterized by a particular type of activity as by an attitude toward it. In the midst of the most sacred presence or activity, we can be driven by fear or competitiveness. It comes as a surprise to find in the gospels that in the very presence of the Christ, the disciples were competing as to who would sit on the right side of Christ in heaven and who would be farther away! The low level of daily life can intrude even when we are in the presence of the Sacred. In the very holy of holies we can think of self-advancement and self-importance.

What Is Our Life For?

However we live our life—in a dull or an excited manner, or in some extraordinary way—the question as to why we live is always there. The three famous sights which Siddhartha Gautama, the Buddha-to-be, saw—namely, an old person, a diseased person, and a dead body—are not so strange to most of us. There is hardly a person who has not seen all of these three sights. But for most of us, it does not create the sort of psychological revolution it did for Siddhartha Gautama. We are not deeply engaged by these sights. I saw the dead body of my older brother who died when he was younger than I am now, and I was deeply moved. But it cannot be said that it left a permanent revolution in my thinking or behavior or general engagement with life. We see people die, even loved ones, but we do not behave as if we too are going to die. We live in the body as if the body were permanent, not subject to death and decay, mistaking the vehicle for the passenger.

There is a story in the Mahabharata in which a celestial being, a *yaksha*, asks the five Pandava brothers in turn, "What is the greatest mystery in the world?" The stakes are high. If they give an unacceptable answer and still attempt to take water from the lake, they will die. All the four younger brothers die and finally it is the oldest brother, Yudhishtra, the son of Dharma, whose response is found acceptable by the yaksha, who then revives all the dead brothers. The greatest mystery, according to the wise Yudhishtra as well as the yaksha, is that even when I see everyone around me die, I do not really believe that I myself am going to die.

There is nothing that Siddhartha saw and experienced that could not be experienced in our daily life. But we lack a vital engagement, a certain kind of intensity, and the sort of passion that he brought to his experience.

Daily Life as Yoga

For our daily life to be a practice leading to the Real, for it to be yoga, an intensity of engagement is needed. There is no recipe for this, but there are stages. We will not seek to be engaged differently unless we become aware of the lack of intensity, of passion, and of meaning in our lives. This is the first requirement. With this recognition, I may begin to blame others or to expect that a change of the situation will make the difference I yearn for, but I need to realize that it is my own relationship with the world and my activities that need to change. My life is not going to be lived by someone else; I must live it myself—it is my opportunity and my challenge.

Gradually, we can begin to recognize that everything is the way it is because there are large-scale forces—to which we subscribe, or which also operate as much inside ourselves as outside—and that these forces have brought us to where we now are. These forces, which are the forces of the status quo, are very large. We begin to understand not only that a radical transformation of our being is necessary but also that such a transformation is not easy, and that we are deeply addicted to the status quo even though we occasionally see the need to be otherwise. St. Paul speaks for all of us, "I cannot even understand my own actions. I do not do what I want to do but what I hate. What happens is that I do, not the good I will to do, but the evil I do not intend" (Romans 7:15, 19). Arjuna asks, "Krishna, what makes a person commit evil, against his own will, as if compelled by force?" (BG 3:36). When we see the force that causes us to repeat ourselves mechanically, we are ready to turn to the part that yearns to be free of this and to undertake a practice.

We become aware that deep down in ourselves there is a contradiction: there is a part that searches for the truth and wishes to emerge into the light, but there is also a part which is quite willing—usually out of fear and ambition—to subscribe to the status quo and to stay in the dark. In Indian mythology, there is a story of the churning of the milky ocean for obtaining amrita, the elixir of Eternal Life. The antigods (daityas) and the gods (*adityas*) are always in conflict. Both of them wish to live forever and have supremacy. They both wish to obtain amrita. The daityas are children of Kashyapa (literally meaning 'vision') and Diti (meaning 'limited'). The adityas have the same father, Kashyapa, but their mother is Aditi ('unlimited', 'vast'). Naturally, the beings of limited vision fight against the beings of vaster vision. Both of these types of being are also within each one of us, representing and strengthening our own downward and upward tendencies. As the myth goes on to say, Vishnu, the highest God, advises the adityas to undertake the churning of the milky ocean for the purpose of obtaining amrita, but he also tells them that they cannot succeed in this churning without involving their unruly cousins, the daityas. Daityas may not have the right vision, but they have enormous energy, and their force is needed for the difficult task of churning. Both aspects of myself are needed for the requisite effort and striving required for churning the sea of consciousness to find what can lead to freedom from the ravages of time.

When we see our situation and we see the need for transformation, we see that we need the support of a practice of yoga, a way to become free of our usual and ordinary limited habits of mind, feeling, and body. Whatever else we might say about it, yoga involves the whole of ourselves—body, mind, and heart. In order to bring about a change, a merciless self-knowledge is necessary, a recognition of all our contradictions, fears, and wishes. For a true self-knowledge, we need to see ourselves in the midst of daily life. It is precisely where we are and where we can begin from. All our life is like a hologram: any little piece of it contains the whole and can reveal the whole. Our gestures, postures, tone of voice, behavior to animals or to neighbours—any of these is a fit subject for investigation and can reveal a great deal about our inner self.

In the shloka of the Bhagavad Gita that was quoted in the very beginning of this essay, we are advised to renounce all our actions to Krishna while being mindful of our deepest self. What is 'Krishna' for us? One of the roots of the word 'krishna' in Sanskrit is *karshati* which means 'that which draws'. 'Krishna' is what ultimately draws us. So, each one of us must ask of ourselves, "What is my Krishna? What is my Ultimate Attractor? What do I love deep down, more than anything else?" We will discover a lack of unity in ourselves; there are at least two of me, in me: one attracted by Krishna and the other attracted by self-importance.

I came out alone on my way to my tryst.
But who is this that follows me in the silent dark?
I move aside to avoid his presence but I escape him not.
He makes the dust rise from the earth with his swagger;
He adds his loud voice to every word that I utter.
He is my own little self, my Lord, he knows no shame;
But I am ashamed to come to thy door in his company.
—*Tagore,* Gitanjali, *poem 30*

Only when we see the two in us can we see the need to struggle with the undisciplined parts of ourselves, so that they can be gradually brought to submit to those parts which have a vaster vision and which see clearly. When we can engage in the struggle willingly and mindfully, we can embark on a journey in which more and more of ourselves becomes integrated in yoga and by yoga.

Thus our ordinary daily life can become a spiritual practice, a true sanyasa, not by renouncing the world, but by renouncing worldliness. It is a form of dying to the world, which in effect is a form of dying to our self, to the usual self which is thoroughly entangled in the forces ruling the world, forces of reward and punishment, of fear and self-importance. The question "How to live with a centered self, integrated by yoga, but at the same time without being self-centered?" becomes more and more interesting, more and more important.

It has often been said by the sages that only when we are willing and able to die to our old self can we be born into a new vision and a new life. There is a profound saying of an ancient Sufi master, echoed in much of sacred literature, which says, "If you die before you die, then you do not die when you die." Krishnamurti in a conversation about life after death said, "The real question is 'Can I die while I am living? Can I die to all my collections—material, psychological, religious?' If you can die to all that, then you'll find out what is there after death. Either there is nothing; absolutely nothing. Or there is something. But you cannot find out until you actually die while living." St. Paul had said "I die daily."

Dying daily is a spiritual practice—a regaining of a sort of innocence, which is quite different from ignorance, akin to openness and humility, an active unknowing. If I allow myself the luxury of not knowing, and if I am not completely full of myself, I can hear the subtle whispers under the noises of the world outside and inside myself. A contemporary sage in India, Sri Anirvan, remarked that the whole world is like a big bazaar in which everyone is shouting at the top of their voice wanting to make their little bargain. A recognition of this can invite us to true metanoia, a turning around, to a new way of being. Otherwise, the momentum of the status quo, abhinivesha in the terminology of Yoga Sutra of Patañjali, persists. Only in moments of real seeing can an action of true vairagya, a disenchantment with the hold of the unreal on our heart, take place. Otherwise, as Wordsworth put it, "Getting and spending, we lay waste our powers."

When the Real calls us, we realize that our attention fluctuates and that we cannot stay attuned to the call for a long time. We begin to understand that we cannot aspire to the steady wisdom of which Krishna speaks without acquiring steady attention. Then the opening sutra in Patañjali's *Yoga Sutra* acquires a practical importance for us: "Yoga is [for the sake of] steadiness of attention" (YS 1:2). Now we can begin the practice of yoga, as if for the first time.

All Action Is Yoga

All these stages are a progressive movement, not away from our ordinary daily life but toward an awakening to and a transformation of that daily life. In the usual situation, we live in a dreamy state of *nishkarma kama*, actionless desiring. The practice of yoga, as it is strongly emphasized by Krishna in the Bhagavad Gita, is for the sake of *nishkama karma*, purposive action without selfish desire. Then the ordinary daily life itself is transformed, because the person who is living it is different. The same cooking and dishwashing, the same lecturing or writing or putting the garbage out is now extraordinary.

All action, all life is yoga. Yoga is relevant here and now, whoever I am, and wherever I am. What I am will change, and I will occupy different places. Yoga is not one specific action, or one particular exercise, or a fixed point of view. Every action, thought or situation can be yoga if it helps to bring about an integration. Each chapter in the Bhagavad Gita ends with a colophon declaring it to be a yoga, including the first chapter, which is called "the yoga of Arjuna's crisis." In the moment of a crisis of conscience, in the midst of despair and a decision not to act resulting from his recognition of the conflict of dharmas at various levels, Arjuna turns to Krishna, who is seated in his heart, as his own highest self. Thus begins Arjuna's apprenticeship in yoga. Krishna is also seated in our heart, and we too can begin our practice of yoga.

Krishna enumerates many definitions of yoga and many characteristics of a yogi, both as a beginner as well as an accomplished practitioner, appropriate to the stage of development of the aspirant. A yogi renounces inaction, then renounces the fruits of action, and then is gradually able to abandon all action except that which is the fulfillment of the will of Krishna, the Highest Being. Yogis are progressively free of dualities such as like-dislike, attachment-revulsion, success-failure, sorrow-pleasure. They are freer and freer of partiality, of desire, fear and anger, selfishness and pride. A yogi takes recourse to buddhi, mindfulness, and more and more acquires a stability of attention which is not unhinged by whatever the theologians, philosophers, or scientists have said or what they will say (BG 2:49–54). Yoga is work well done (BG 2:50); it is the breaking of an attachment to past suffering (BG 6:23), and it is everything that leads us to our Krishna, our Highest Attractor, the sole signifier of significance in our life.

Whatever you do, whatever you eat, whatever sacrifice you undertake, whatever charity you give, whatever efforts you make, do all that as an offering unto Me" (BG 9.27).

And Yoga Is No Action

After much searching, striving, effort, responsibilities, and action, there is the call to abandon all doing, a complete surrender to the Highest Being (BG 18:66). In this state of total attention, of pure awareness, a yogi does not decide to do this or that. Right and compassionate action is a natural outcome of this state. It is not a state of inaction, but of nonegoistic action. I do not do it, but it is done through me or in me. As the *Tao te Ching* says, "The sage does nothing, but nothing is left undone." This recognition is expressed in another tradition, where Christ says, "I am not myself the source of the words I speak: it is the Father who dwells in me doing His own work" (John 14:10). Meister Eckhart: "What we receive in contemplation, we give out in love." Reverting to the Bhagavad Gita, seeing that gunas act upon gunas, a yogi realizes that he does nothing at all (13:29).

There is a mystery here. Not the kind of mystery that can be solved by the discovery of a missing clue by some clever sleuthing. It is a mystery not because something is missing, but more because it is overfull. It cannot be solved by our usual rational mind, but we can contact a level of being—of body, mind, and heart—where it is dissolved. Solving this mystery, much as responding to a koan in Zen, is not a matter of articulating a published solution. In a breakthrough of consciousness another level of being is contacted. This other being is naturally reflected in the way we talk, stand, or walk. Uday Shankar, the greatest Indian dancer in the twentieth century, felt hesitant even toward the end of his life to perform the dance he called "the walk of the Buddha after his enlightenment." Finally he did dance it, as an offering, a summation of his entire life's practice and understanding of dance, the yoga of his life.

The solution to the mystery of acting while doing nothing, or of doing nothing while engaged in vigorous action, is not to be found in this or that description. The solution is inherent in a fundamental transformation of consciousness. Daily life is not only the place of spiritual practice, it is the goal of all spiritual practice. We may understand something in a monastery or in a cave or behind a tree, but we must return to where the ordinary forces are at play and where we must have our action for the sake of the world. Even after he had seen the great form of the Godhead, a vision not vouchsafed to many in the history of the universe, Arjuna had to fight in the battle that ensued.

Krishna said in the Mahabharata that the choice a person faces is not between war and lack of war, or struggle and lack of struggle. The only choice is between struggle at one level or at another. We need to struggle in our world, in our daily life, against our own egos. If we are free at our present level of existence, then we shall have to struggle at other levels. After all, even the angels or the devas have egos, and they too have to struggle. A real practice of yoga will not take us away from the battle in the world, from daily life.. It will lead us to an understanding of how to be engaged in the battle and yet still be above it. This is what Krishna says about such yogis:

> *Involved, they seem like onlookers,*
> *The various forces of nature do not disturb them.*
> *They know that this is all a play of forces.*
> *They are firm, unshaken. (BG 14:22)*

Glossary of Selected Sanskrit and Pali Words

Many Sanskrit and some Pali words have been used in the present volume. Often, the nearest meaning of the word is given in the text. However, it is useful to append this glossary for a quick reference. In general, in the text the appropriate diacritical marks have been left out and phonetic spellings have been supplied. These words are given below in parenthesis with the diacritical marks.

abhinivesha (abhiniveśa): momentum to continue in the state one is in

abhyasa (abhyāsa): practice, repetition

aditya (āditya): truth

Aditya (āditya): god, the Sun god, child of Aditi (vast, unlimited) and Kashyapa (vision)

Advaitin: proponent of Advaita Vedānta

ahamkara (ahaṁkāra): egotism, sense of self, pride; literally, "I am the doer"

ahimsa (ahiṁsā): nonviolation, nonviolence

amrita: eternal life, also nectar of eternal life

asana (āsana): posture; one of the five external limbs of yoga according to Patañjali

asmita (asmitā): egoism, "I am this"

asura: antigod, demon, an evil spirit

Atman (ātman, often used in the nominative form ***ātmā)***: Self, Spirit, soul, the deepest part of a person

Aum: same as *Om*

avatara (avatāra): descent of a deity; incarnation—particularly of Viṣṇu, the maintainer of cosmic order

avidya (avidyā): ignorance, illusion, sometimes personified as *Māyā*

Bhagavad Gita (Bhagavad-gītā, Bhagavad Gītā): Song of the Blessed One; perhaps the single most important work to originate from India. It is a part of the great epic *Mahābhārata*; date range 600–200 BCE.

bhakti: devotion, adoration, worship, love

bhava (bhāva): natural state, character, or quality

bodhi: perfect knowledge or wisdom (by which a person becomes buddha)

Brahma (Brahmā): first of the triad of personalized gods, *Brahmā—Viṣṇu—Śiva*; Universal Spirit manifested as Creator, the Great Being

Brahman: Godhead, *Deitas*, Absolute, self-existent nonpersonal Spirit, the Ultimate Reality; literally, Vastness

brahmanda (brahmāṇḍa): cosmos, "egg of Brahman"

brahmin (brāhmaṇa): one who has sacred knowledge; one belonging to the first of the four castes

Buddha: Awakened, awake, enlightened, liberated; used as a proper name of the historical Siddhartha Gautama

buddhi: soul, will, intellect, integrated intelligence, understanding

chakra: center of energy related to the human organism

chitta (citta): Mind, consciousness

Daitya : demon, anti-god, child of Diti (limited) and Kashyapa (vision)

darshana (darśana): point of view, perspective, school of philosophy

deva: god

Dhammapada: an early Buddhist document discussing the chief values of life and the path which leads to enlightenment

dharma: law, order, responsibility for the maintenance of order, duty, religion, righteousness, obligation, teaching

dharmashastra (dharmaśāstra): classical texts in which are found the requirements of dharma

dharana (dhāraṇā): absorption, deep devotion; one of the three internal limbs of Patañjali Yoga

dhyana (dhyāna): meditation, contemplation; one of the three internal limbs of Yoga. *Dhyana* becomes *Ch'an* in Chinese, *Sôn* in Korean, and *Zen* in Japanese

dukkha (the Sanskrit equivalent of this Pali word is ***duḥkha***): suffering, anguish, affliction, angst, sorrow

dvesha (dveṣa): aversion, dislike, hate

guna (guṇa): strand, constituent; the three gunas—*satva, rajas, tamas*—are the three fundamental constituents of the whole of *Prakriti* (Nature) even at the most subtle level

Ishvara (Īśvara): God, the supreme Being, personal Deity

jiva (jīva): the individual soul

jñana (jñāna): wisdom, sacred knowledge (as distinct from *vijñāna* which is profane knowledge, science)

kaivalya: aloneness, highest state of consciousness according to Patañjali Yoga

kala (kāla): time; also identified with *Yāma* (Lord of death as well as of dharma); the root word is *kal,* which means to calculate or enumerate

kama (kāma): wish, desire, longing; *Kāma* is god of sexual love or desire

karma: act, action, work; result, effect; *law of karma* (cause and effect) is cosmic, i.e., applied to moral, and psychological as well as physical spheres

klesha (kleśa): obstacle, impediment

Krishna (Kṛṣṇa): the teacher in the Bhagavad Gita, the eighth incarnation of Viṣhṇu

kshatriya (kṣatriya): member of the warrior or administrator class

kshetra (kṣetra): field

kshudra brahmanda (kṣudrā brahmāṇḍa): small egg of Brahma, microcosmos

linga: mark, sign, trace; Shiva-linga is the phallus of Shiva, *linga sharira* is the subtle body which does not die at the death of the physical body

Mahabharata (Mahābhārata): great epic which is found the Bhagavad Gītā

manas: lower mind, reason; faculty by which objects of sense affect *buddhi*

mantra: 'mind-instrument'; special sounds usually given by a teacher to the disciple for recitation

maya (māyā): illusion, unreality, deception, power; from the same root as 'measure'; *Māyā* is illusion personified, identified with *Prakriti*

moksha (mokṣa): unconditioned and uncaused freedom, liberation

mukti: freedom, liberation, final beatitude; same as *mokṣa*

nirvana (nirvāṇa, nibbāna in Pali***)***: extinction of *tanhā* (selfish craving), the highest felicity

nivritti (nivṛtti): returning to the source, withdrawal, tendency opposite to *pravritti* (*pravṛtti*)

niyama: restraint, control; one of the five outer limbs of Yoga

Om: primordial vibration, most sacred syllable; same as *Aum*

paramatma: the universal Self, God

prajña (prajñā): insight, wisdom, understanding

prakrita (prākṛta): natural, unrefined, vulgar, common

prakriti (prakṛti): nature; materiality; sometimes same as *māyā*

prana (prāṇa): subtle energy, breath; equivalent to *Chi* (*Qi*) in Chinese thought

pranayama (prāṇāyāma): regulation of *prāṇa*, breath control; one of the five outer limbs of Yoga

pratyahara (pratyāhāra): drawing back the senses; one of the five outer limbs of Yoga

pravritti (pravṛtti): manifestation, outward and expansive tendency, as opposed to *nivritti* (*nivṛtti*)

purusha (puruṣa): person, primeval man, Supreme Being, also identified with *Atman* and *Brahman*

raga (rāga): liking, attraction, melody; opposite of *dveṣa*

rajas: the *guṇa* of passion and activity

Ramayana: great epic, the story of Rāma

Rig Veda (Ṛg Veda): the oldest of the four Vedas and the oldest text in any Indo-European language; the oldest parts may date back to 3000 BCE

rita (ṛta): cosmic order

sadhaka (sādhaka): aspirant, practitioner

sadhana (sādhanā): practice, effort, quest

samadhi (samādhi): putting together, joining, synthesis, composure; integration; profound meditation; the eighth and last state of Yoga

Samkhya (sāṁkhya): one of the important schools of philosophy in India, often closely associated with Yoga

samsara (saṁsāra): world, secular life, worldly illusion; the circuit of mundane existence; the cosmic flux

samkalpa (saṁkalpa): imagination, self-will, or desire-will

samskara (saṁskāra): impression, influence

samyama (saṁyama): discipline, steady attention which is a combination of *dhyāna*, *dhāraṇā* and *samādhi* in Yoga of Patañjali

sanatana (sanātana): eternal, immemorial

sanyasa (sanyāsa): renunciation

Sanskrit: name of the sacred language of India

Sanskrita (saṁskṛta): well-formed, perfected, refined, educated

sat: being

satva: the *guṇa* of lucidity and mindfulness

satya: truth

shakti (śakti): energy, power, the feminine counterpart of *Shiva*

Shankara (Śaṁkara): one of the greatest philosophers of India who propounded *Advaita* (nondual) *Vedānta*

sharira (śarīra): body (including the mind and emotions)

Shiva (Śiva): auspicious; lord of sleep; third of the Hindu triad of personalized Gods, *Brahma—Viṣṇu–Śiva*; lord of transformation and of destruction and reassimilation

shraddha (śraddhā): faith, reverential belief

shruti (śruti): that which has been heard, revelation

shudra (śūdra): worker, laborer, one of the four castes

shunyata (śūnyatā): zeroness, emptiness, the doctrine that anything in isolation from the whole is insignificant and nonexistent

siddhi: power, accomplishment

smriti (smṛti): that which is remembered, tradition

sutra (sūtra): literally, thread; a short rule or aphorism (as used in Sanskrit texts)

svabhava (svabhāva): inner calling, essential nature, own being

svadharma: *dharma* (obligation) corresponding to one's *svabhāva*

svakarma: *karma* (action) corresponding to one's *svabhāva*

tamas: the *guṇa* corresponding to inertia, sloth, and stability

tanha (tanhā in Pali, ***trishnā*** in Sanskrit***)***: selfishness, egoistic craving, desire

tapas: heat; spiritual austerity, penance, effort

tapasya (tapasyā): effort, sustained practice, austerity

Tathagata (Tathāgata): epithet of the Buddha; literally, 'thus gone', or one who has found the Truth

tirtha (tīrtha): sacred ford, holy water, place of pilgrimage

turiya (turīya): the fourth [state of consciousness], as distinguished from dreamless sleep, dreaming, and waking

Upanishad (upaniṣad): important sacred writings of the Hindus, usually philosophical in nature. These constitute the concluding portion of the Vedas, and number over 200 different works, dating between 800 and 500 BCE. Among the most important Upaniṣads are: *Iśa*, *Kena*, *Kaṭha*, *Muṇḍaka*, *Praśna*, *Māṇḍūkya*, *Taittirīya*, *Aitareya*, *Chāndogya*, *Bṛhad-āraṇayaka*, *Śvetāśvatara*, and the *Maitrī*.

vairagya (vairāgya): detachment, withdrawal from the world of reward and punishment

vaishya (vaiśya): a member of the merchant caste

vasana (vāsanā): innate and deep tendency

Veda: the most sacred literature of the Hindus; knowledge. There are four *Vedas*, the oldest being the *Rig* (*Ṛg*) *Veda*, composed around 1500 BCE or before.

Vedanta (vedānta): end of knowledge; end of the Veda; most influential school of philosophy in India

vidya (vidyā): mental knowledge, wisdom

Vishnu (Viṣṇu): second of the Hindu triad of Gods, *Brahmā—Viṣṇu—Śiva*; the preserver and the sustainer

viveka: discernment

vrata: vow

vritti (vṛtti): modification, fluctuation, tendency

yajña: sacrifice; a sacrificial rite or ceremony; an exchange between levels

Yama: Lord of death and of *dharma*; yama: one of the five outer limbs of Yoga

yoga: integration, union, the art of yoking, joining, attaching; meditation with the aim of union with *Ishvara* or the Supreme Spirit; any path for such union

Yoga Sutra (Yoga Sūtra): the most important text of yoga, attributed to the great sage Patañjali

Bibliography

Alighieri, Dante. *The Divine Comedy*. Translated by John Ciardi. New York: New American Library, 2003.

Aurobindo, Sri. *The Integral Yoga*. Twin Lakes, WI: Lotus Press, 1993.
———. *The Upanishads*. Twin Lakes, WI: Lotus Press, 1996.

Austin, G. *The Indian Constitution: Cornerstone of a Nation*. Oxford: Clarendon Press, 1966.

Case, Margaret, ed. *The Inner Journey: Views from the Hindu Tradition*. Sandpoint, ID: Morning Light Press, 2007.

Coomaraswamy, A. K. and Sister Nivedita. *Hindus and Buddhists: Myths and Legends*. London: Bracken Books, 1985.

Davies, Oliver, ed. and trans. *Meister Eckhart: Selected Writings*. London: Penguin, 1994.

Deshpande, P. Y. *The Authentic Yoga: A Fresh Look at Patanjali's Yoga Sutras with a New Translation, Notes and Comments*. London: Rider, 1978.

Desikachar, T. K. V. *The Heart of Yoga*. Rochester, VT: Inner Traditions, 1999.

Einstein, Albert. *Ideas and Opinions*. New York: Crown, 1954.
———. *Out of My Later Years*. New York: Philosophical Library, 1950.

Eliade, Mircea. *Patañjali and Yoga.* Translated by Charles Lam Markmann. New York: Schocken Books, 1975.

———. *Yoga: Immortality and Freedom.* Translated by Willard R. Trask. Princeton: Princeton University Press, 1969.

Eliot, Thomas Sterns. *Four Quartets.* London: Faber and Faber, 1996.

Feuerstein, Georg. *The Yoga-Sutra of Patañjali: A New Translation and Commentary.* Rochester, VT: Inner Traditions, 1989.

Harris, R. Blaine, ed. *Neoplatonism and Indian Thought.* Albany: State University of New York Press, 1982.

Gurdjieff, G. I. *Beelzebub's Tales to His Grandson.* New York: Harcourt Brace, 1950; London: E. P. Dutton, 1964; rev. ed. New York: Viking Arkana, 1992.

———. *Life Is Real Only Then, When 'I Am'.* New York: Elsevier-Dutton, 1981.

———. *Meetings with Remarkable Men.* New York: E. P. Dutton, 1963.

———. *Views from the Real World.* New York: E. P. Dutton, 1973.

Jacobs, Hans. *Western Psychotherapy and Hindu Sadhana.* London: Allen & Unwin, 1961.

Kabir. *One Hundred Poems of Kabir.* Translated by Rabindranath Tagore, assisted by Evelyn Underhill. London: Macmillan, 1967.

Krishnamurti, J. *Commentaries on Living.* I. Edited by D. Rajagopal. Wheaton, IL: Quest Books, 1967.

Majumdar, R. C., ed. *The History and the Culture of the Indian People.* Vol. 10, *British Paramountcy and Indian Renaissance.* Bombay: Bharatiya Vidya Bhavan, 1965.

Miller, Barbara Stoler, trans. *The Bhagavad Gita.* New York: Bantam, 1986.
———, trans. *Yoga–Discipline of Freedom: The Yoga Sutra Attributed to Patañjali.* Berkeley, CA: University of California Press, 1996.

The New English Bible with the Apocrypha. Oxford University Press and Cambridge University Press, 1970.

Nikhilananda, Swami, trans. *The Gospel of Shri Ramakrishna.* New York: Ramakrishna-Vivekananda Center, 1955.
———. *The Principal Upanishads.* Hollywood, CA: Vedanta Press, 2003.

Novak, Philip, ed. *The Inner Journey: Views from the Buddhist Tradition.* Sandpoint, ID: Morning Light Press, 2005.

Ouspensky, P. D. *In Search of the Miraculous: Fragments of an Unknown Teaching.* Orlando, FL: Harcourt, 2001.

Pascal, Blaise. *Pensées.* Translated by H. F. Stewart. New York: Modern Library, 1967.

Prabhavananda, Swami and C. Isherwood, trans. *How to Know God: The Yoga Aphorisms of Patañjali.* New York: New American Library, 1969.

Radhakrishnan, S., ed. and trans. *The Principal Upanishads.* London: Allen & Unwin. 1953.

Radhakrishnan, S., and P. T. Raju, eds. *The Concept of Man.* London: George Allen & Unwin, 1966.

Ravindra, R. *Centered Self without Being Self-Centered: Remembering Krishnamurti.* Sandpoint, ID: Morning Light Press, 2003.
———. *The Gospel of John in the Light of Indian Mysticism.* Rochester, VT: Inner Traditions, 2004. [Earlier published as *The Yoga of the Christ* and as *Christ the Yogi.*]

———. *Heart Without Measure: Gurdjieff Work with Madame de Salzmann.* Sandpoint, ID: Morning Light Press, 2004.

———. *Krishnamurti: Two Birds on One Tree.* Wheaton, IL: Quest Books, 1995.

———. *Pilgrim Without Boundaries.* Sandpoint, ID: Morning Light Press, 2003.

———. *Science and the Sacred.* Wheaton, IL: Quest Books, 2002.

———. *Whispers from the Other Shore: Spiritual Search—East and West.* Halifax, Nova Scotia: Shaila Press, 2000.

———. *Yoga and the Teaching of Krishna.* Adyar, Chennai, India: Theosophical Publishing House, 1998.

Sardananda, Swami. *Shri Shri Ramakrishna Lilaprasang.* Calcutta: Udobodhan Office, 1955.

Singh, Khushwant. "Sikhism." In *The Encyclopedia of Religion*, Vol. 13. Edited by Mircea Eliade et al. New York: Macmillan, 1987.

Smith, Huston. *The World's Religions.* San Francisco: Harper, 1991.

Tagore, Rabindranath. *Gitanjali (Song Offerings).* London: Macmillan, 1913.

Thurman, Robert, trans. *The Tibetan Book of the Dead.* New York: Bantam, 1994.

Valmiki. *Ramayana.* Translated by William Buck. Berkley: University of California Press, 1976.

Varenne, Jean. *Yoga and the Hindu Tradition.* Translated by Derek Coltman. Chicago: University of Chicago Press, 1976.

Zaehner, R. C., ed. *The Bhagavad Gita.* New York: Oxford University Press, 1969.

Zimmer, H. *Myths and Symbols in Indian Art and Civilization.* Edited by Joseph Campbell. Princeton: Princeton University Press, 1974.

Index

BOOKS OF RELATED INTEREST FROM NAB

THE HINDU MIND : Fundamentals of Hindu Religion and Philosophy for All Ages—*Bansi Pandit*

The Hindu Mind provides an excellent introduction to the historical, philosophical, ritualistic, social, and ethical dimensions of Hinduism. The major contribution of the book is that it shows the interconnections among these diverse dimensions. The author brings to the people the key concepts such as Brahman, karma, dharma, maya and samskara, which constitute the foundational beliefs of Hinduism.

ISBN: 978-81-7822-007-9

EASTERN SPIRITUALITY FOR MODERN LIFE : Exploring Buddhism, Hinduism, Taoism and Tantra —*David Pond*

Each religion might very well see a separate aspect of truth and be blind to the others. It is clear that our shrinking world requires us to step outside of our separatist ways and seek to better understand each other. It is in this spirit that this book is written. We are all here together; there are no good religions, nor bad religions, just different religions.

ISBN: 978-81-7822-199-1

AYURVEDIC YOGA THERAPY —*Mukunda Stiles*

"By marrying the sister sciences of Yoga and Ayurveda, Mukunda steers a way from an increasing tendency to 'medicalize' yoga therapy. Instead of offering prescriptive recommendations for specific medical diagnoses, he presents sequences of Vinyasa and pranayama suited to the various Ayurvedic body types. Yoga therapists and practitioners using this book can access a deeper level of preventative self-care, attuning to the rhythm and balance of each individual.

ISBN: 978-81-7822-343-8

HIMALAYAN MYSTICISM : Shiva's Disc To Cut Asunder and Open the Mystic Heart—*Ralph Nataraj*

The book not only passes information, but very much expands the consciousness of the readers. The author does that in a brilliant manner. Those who learn with an open mind and heart are often swept away by waves of inner joy and beauty.

The book is, without doubt, unusual because it aims to transform its readers from ordinary human beings to sadhakas. It is spiritual, has depth and a clear message for the readers: transform yourselves.

ISBN: 978-81-7822-289-9 (HB)
ISBN: 978-81-7822-290-5 (PB)

WHAT IS KARMA —*Paul Brunton*

"Karma" is a household word by now. But how many of us actually know what it means? Here is a refreshing, positive view of karma, from one of the 20th century's most perceptive students of how timeless wisdom enhances contemporary life. He explains:- What karma is - How it works - Its relation to forgiveness, freedom, and enlightenment - How to get it working for you. Karma is simply a power of the Universal Mind to effect adjustment, to restore equilibrium, and to bring about compensatory balance. Karma is a self-moving force, nobody, human or superhuman, has to operate it.

ISBN: 978-81-7822-331-5

FINDING SOUL IN WORK AND LIFE :
—*Prafulla Raval & Vasant Raval*

Spirituality transcends religion, rituals, dogmas and rules. The authors here try to explain in a systematic manner the meaning and role of spirituality in lives and how to get it, trickle by trickle, untile the bucket is full. The authors hope that you will understand, not just receive and you will grasp the *why* part of the puzzle as much as the *how*.

ISBN: 978-81-7822-353-7

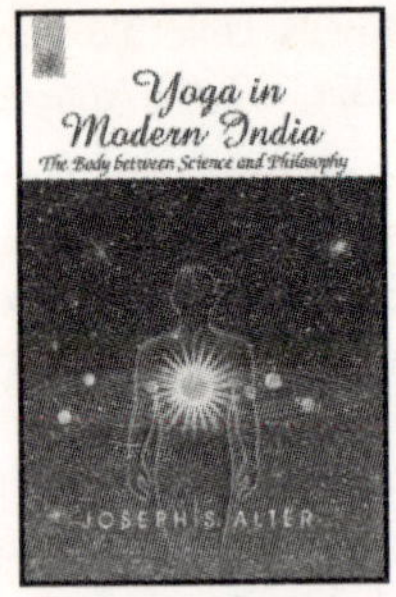

YOGA IN MODERN INDIA : The Body between Science and Philosophy —*Joseph S. Alter*

Based on extensive ethnographic research and an analysis of both ancient and modern texts, *Yoga in Modern India* challenges this popular view by examining the history of yoga, focusing on its emergence in modern India and its dramatically changing form and significance in the twentieth century. Much of the book is quite accessible to general reader, and many of Alter's more theoretical and analytical interpretations of modern understandings of yoga, health, medicine, the body and truth claims are novel and stimulating.

ISBN: 978-81-7822-324-7

YOGA SUTRAS OF PATANJALI —*Baba Hari Dass*

Only a saint with deep spiritual experience is qualified to write a commentary on the *Yoga-Sūtras* or any other text of the meditative tradition. All of these texts have emerged from a *ṛṣi's* state of *samādhi.* Only one sitting within the heights and spans of their all-transcending, all-containing horizons can hope to have a glimpse of their truths. Venerable Baba Hari Dass has been guided by the Himalayan Masters like Baba Haiḍa Khan. He is steeped in his own Vaiṣṇava tradition, he has kept total silence for well over five decades, while still establishing his flourishing Ashram in California where he has guided thousands of students in the spritual path.

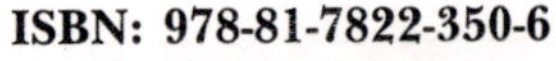
ISBN: 978-81-7822-350-6

PERSPECTIVES : The Timeless Way of Wisdom THE NOTE BOOKS OF PAUL BRUNTON (VOL.1)
—*Elisabeth Kubler-Ross*

Perspectives is an inspiring insight into the essence of East-West spiritual philosophy. Going to the heart of virtually every aspect of the spiritual quest, it introduces a major series: The Notebooks of Paul Brunton.

"His 'Notebooks' provide a veritable treasure trove of philosophic-spiritual wisdom."

ISBN: 978-81-7822-338-4